冨樫義博

I got married (details in volume 5).

Yoshihiro Togashi

Yoshihiro Togashi's manga career began in 1986 at the age of 20, when he won the coveted Osamu Tezuka Award for new manga artists. He debuted in the Japanese **Weekly Shonen Jump** magazine in 1989 with the romantic comedy **Tende Shôwaru Cupid**. From 1990 to 1994 he wrote and drew the hit manga **YuYu Hakusho**, which was followed by the dark comedy science-fiction series **Level E,** and finally this adventure series **Hunter x Hunter**. In 1999 he married the manga artist Naoko Takeuchi.

HUNTER X HUNTER Volume 4
SHONEN JUMP Manga Edition

STORY AND ART BY
YOSHIHIRO TOGASHI

English Adaptation/Gary Leach
Translation/Lillian Olsen
Touch-up Art & Lettering/Mark Griffin
Design/Amy Martin
Editor/Pancha Diaz

Printed in the U.S.A.

Published by VIZ Media, LLC
P.O. Box 77010
San Francisco, CA 94107

10 9 8
First printing, August 2005
Eighth printing, January 2021

HUNTER × HUNTER

ハンター × ハンター

Story & Art by
Yoshihiro Togashi

Volume 4

CHARACTERS

The Story Thus Far

GON DREAMS OF BECOMING A HUNTER LIKE HIS FATHER, AND HAS APPLIED FOR THE ULTRA-DIFFICULT LICENSING EXAM. HE'S REACHED THE FOURTH PHASE, THE OBJECT OF WHICH IS TO ACQUIRE I.D. BADGES FROM OTHER APPLICANTS, TOTALING SIX POINTS. ONE'S OWN BADGE IS WORTH THREE POINTS, ONE'S TARGET'S IS WORTH THREE POINTS, AND ALL OTHERS ARE EACH WORTH ONE POINT. GON'S TARGET—THE DEADLY HISOKA!! TAKING A CUE FROM OBSERVATIONS OF FISHING BIRDS, GON HIDES AND LIES IN WAIT TO TAKE ADVANTAGE OF THE MOMENT HISOKA GOES FOR HIS OWN PREY. MEANWHILE, KURAPIKA AND LEORIO FORM AN ALLIANCE, AND KURAPIKA'S TARGET SOON YIELDS HIS BADGE. HOWEVER, HISOKA'S ON THE PROWL TO NAIL DOWN TWO MORE POINTS, AND IS SNEAKING UP ON THEM!

Gon

OUR HERO ASPIRES TO BECOME A HUNTER AND REUNITE WITH HIS FATHER!

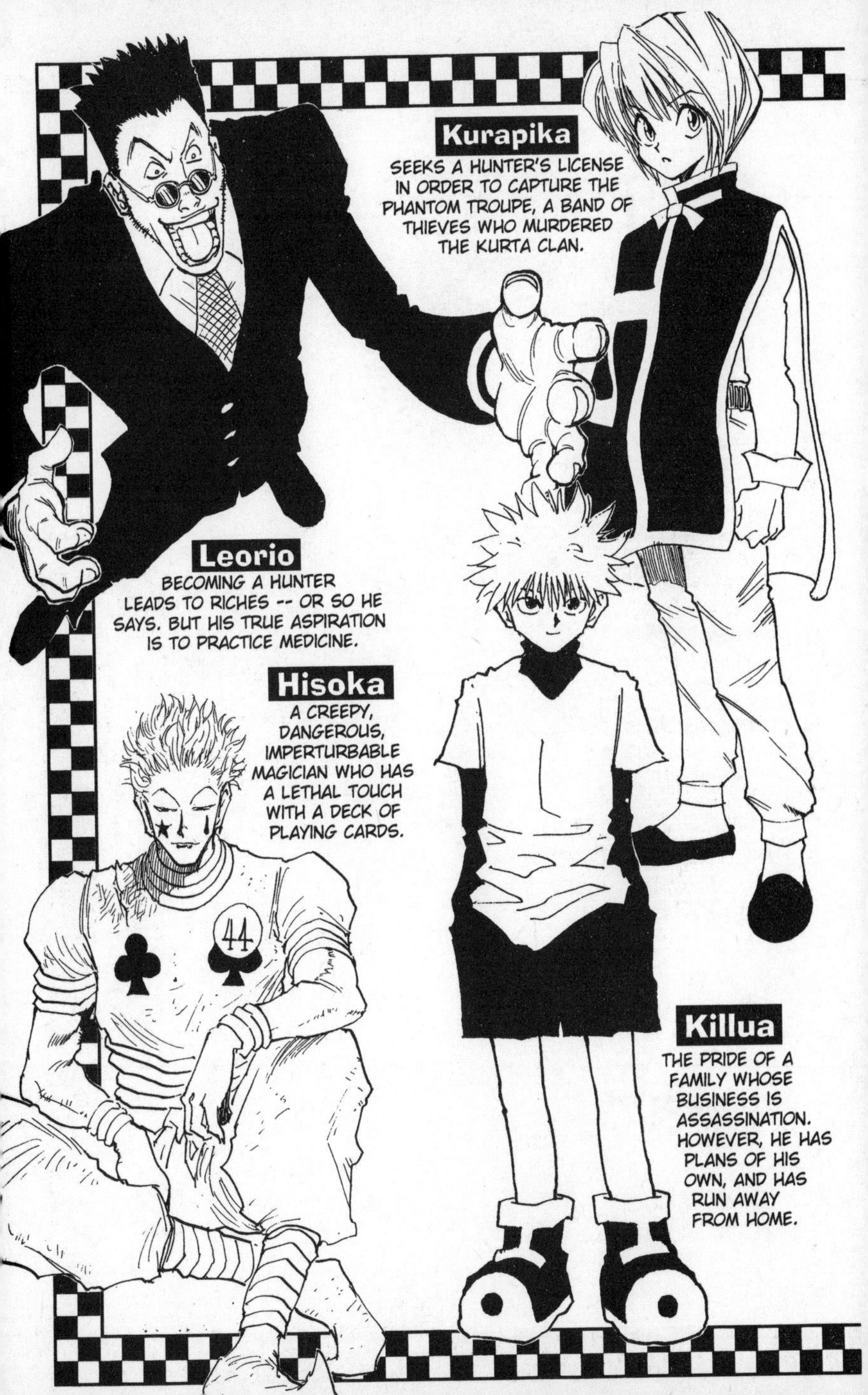
Kurapika
SEEKS A HUNTER'S LICENSE IN ORDER TO CAPTURE THE PHANTOM TROUPE, A BAND OF THIEVES WHO MURDERED THE KURTA CLAN.
Leorio
BECOMING A HUNTER LEADS TO RICHES -- OR SO HE SAYS. BUT HIS TRUE ASPIRATION IS TO PRACTICE MEDICINE.
Hisoka
A CREEPY, DANGEROUS, IMPERTURBABLE MAGICIAN WHO HAS A LETHAL TOUCH WITH A DECK OF PLAYING CARDS.
44
Killua
THE PRIDE OF A FAMILY WHOSE BUSINESS IS ASSASSINATION. HOWEVER, HE HAS PLANS OF HIS OWN, AND HAS RUN AWAY FROM HOME.

Volume 4

CONTENTS

Chapter 27
A Volatile Situation

Chapter 27
A Volatile Situation

READ THIS WAY

...

OKAY, THE MOMENT HISOKA ATTACKS, I'LL SNATCH HIS BADGE!!

IT'S MY BEST SHOT! MY ONLY SHOT!

...!!

BUT I CAN'T DO IT!!
THIS ISN'T ABOUT POINTS! I HAVE TO FIGURE OUT HOW TO HELP THEM!

!!

HELLO. ♦

HISOKA!!

I NEED TWO MORE BADGES TO PASS. ♣
MAY I HAVE YOURS?

SAY WHAT?
YOU THINK WE'LL JUST HAND YOU OUR..?!
HOLD ON!

YOU SAID, "TWO MORE BADGES."
SO NEITHER ONE OF US IS YOUR PRIMARY TARGET.

THAT'S NOT THE ISSUE. ♠
ARE YOU GOING TO GIVE ME YOUR BADGES... OR NOT?
THAT DEPENDS.

FOUR BADGES ARE ON THE TABLE HERE.
I HAVE MY OWN, AND THAT OF MY TARGET.
AND ONE ONE-POINTER.
AND LEORIO'S BADGE. THAT'S FOUR.
ONLY **TWO** OF THESE MIGHT REPRESENT YOUR SPECIFIC TARGET.
MY **OWN** BADGE...
...OR THE ONE THAT, TO **US**, IS WORTH ONLY ONE POINT.

44
LEORIO'S I.D. NUMBER IS 403...
...AND HE WAS TONPA'S TARGET. TONPA'S NUMBER...
...IS 16--AND HE WAS **MY** TARGET.
SINCE WE'RE EACH THE TARGET OF ONLY ONE OTHER...
16

READ THIS WAY

FLICK
SNAP
HEH
HEH
HEH
HEH.
♥

WHAT'S *YOUR* I.D. NUMBER?

404.

THAT SETTLES THAT. ♣
YOU'RE NOT MY TARGET. ♠

VERY WELL. ♦

I'LL TAKE YOUR ONE-POINTER. ♣
ODDS ARE AGAINST IT... BUT, HEY, I *MIGHT* GET LUCKY. ♦

FWIP

I'LL LEAVE IT HERE.

NO PROBLEM. ♥
YOU GO... I'LL STAY RIGHT HERE. ♦
FFFT

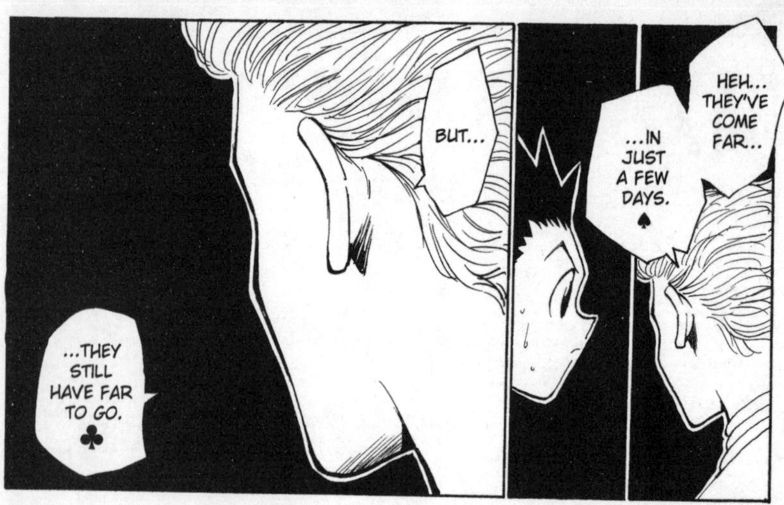
HEH... THEY'VE COME FAR...
...IN JUST A FEW DAYS. ♠
BUT...
...THEY STILL HAVE FAR TO GO. ♣

FUNNY HOW UNRIPE FRUIT...
...ALWAYS HAS SUCH A PARTICULAR APPEAL. ♥

118
HMM.. TOO BAD. ♥
NO LUCK *THIS* ROUND. ♦

ON WITH THE HUNT. ♣

PLIP
WHEW!

THAT LEAVES ME JUST ONE MORE CHANCE, THOUGH.
THE NEXT TIME HISOKA CATCHES A SCENT, I'LL...
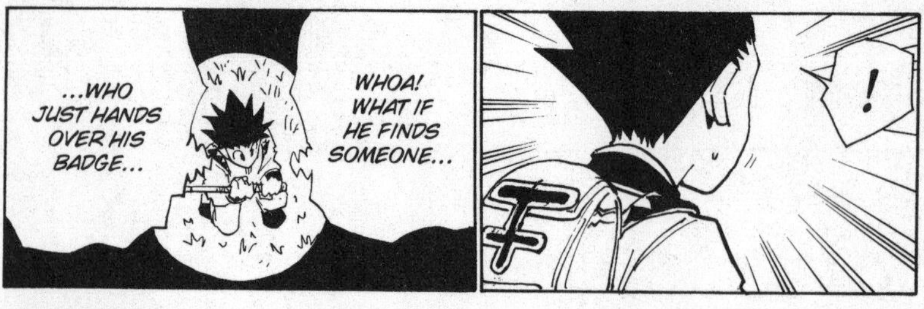
!
WHOA! WHAT IF HE FINDS SOMEONE...
...WHO JUST HANDS OVER HIS BADGE...

...WITHOUT PUTTING UP A FIGHT? IT COULD HAPPEN!
IN FACT, IT'S PRETTY DARN LIKELY! I NEVER...
BRRR

EEP!

SKEEK!
SHIVER
...
I'M EDGY, SCARED... I DON'T LIKE IT HERE!!
ALL THIS BLOODLUST...
SCREECH!
SCREECH!
TREMBLE
TREMBLE
...

NOW LOOK WHAT THEY'VE DONE. ♠
THEY HAD TO GO AND GET ME... STIRRED UP. ♣
GOT TO KEEP A GRIP. ♦

WELL, ONWARD. ◆
SHIFF
HE'S GOING FOR IT!!

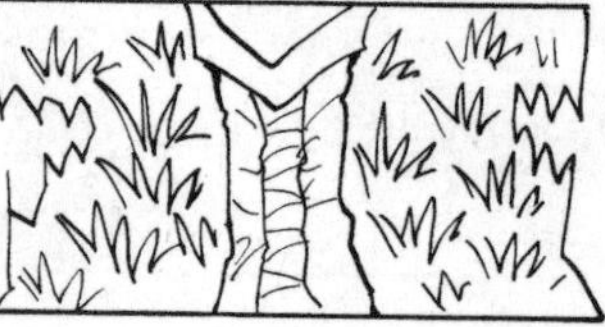
THE EXTREME BLOODLUST IS GONE, BUT...
...BY THE LOOK ON HIS FACE, HE'S NOT ONE TO **TRIFLE WITH** RIGHT NOW.
THE NEXT PERSON HE COMES ACROSS...
...HE'LL **ATTACK**, WHETHER THE OTHER PERSON SURRENDERS OR **NOT**!

READ THIS WAY

THERE'S THE VICTIM!!

HISOKA'S NOT MORE THAN A MINUTE BEHIND...

...SO I GOTTA **HURRY!**

IT'LL BE **OVER IN A FLASH,** IF THE PAST IS ANY INDICATION!

I HAVE TO BE THERE FIRST!!

READ THIS WAY

THIS IS WHERE THEY'LL BE!!

SHOOOSH

Chapter 28
A Huge Favor

Chapter 28
A Huge Favor
FWISH
FWISH
HERE WE GO!!!

...!

OKAY!!
COME GIT ME!
HE'LL FIGHT! GOOD... I THINK!

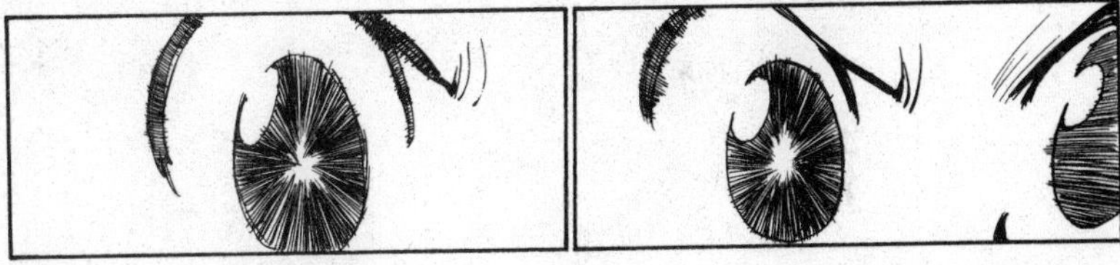

RIIIP

44
FLINK
44

SWIP
SHUFF

READ THIS WAY

SHOOF
SHOOF
SHOOF

HUFF!
HUFF!

BUPPA
BUPPA
BUPPA
BUPPA

I... DID IT!
I GOT...

...HISOKA'S BADGE!!

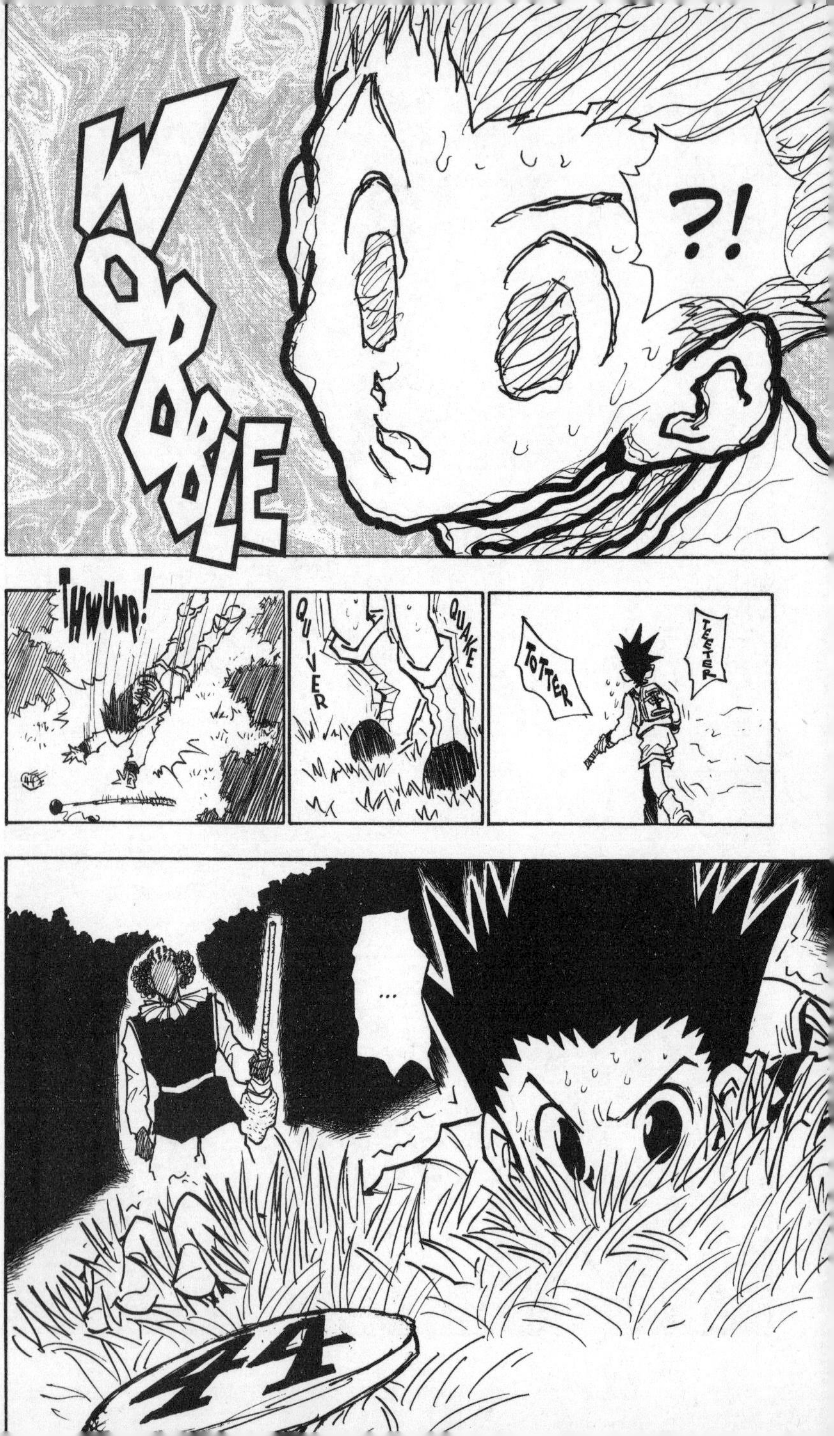

?!

WOBBLE

...

44

SEVEN THOUSAND TIMES.
SUFF
YOU HAVE ANY IDEA WHAT THAT SIGNIFIES?
44

THE NUMBER OF CHANCES I HAD TO NAIL YOU BEFORE NOW...
...AND THE PRACTICE CASTS YOU MADE TO IMPROVE YOUR ACCURACY.
POIT

YOU LEFT YOURSELF OPEN ALL THAT TIME...
...BUT YOUR EFFORTS DESERVED RESPECT.

THAT LAST CAST WAS A REAL STUNNER.
405
SKILL'S ONE THING, THOUGH, AND CAUTION ANOTHER.
44
405

BETTER LUCK NEXT TIME.
FFFT

UNH!

DAMMIT...

!

SHUFF
SHUFF

NICE WORK, KID.

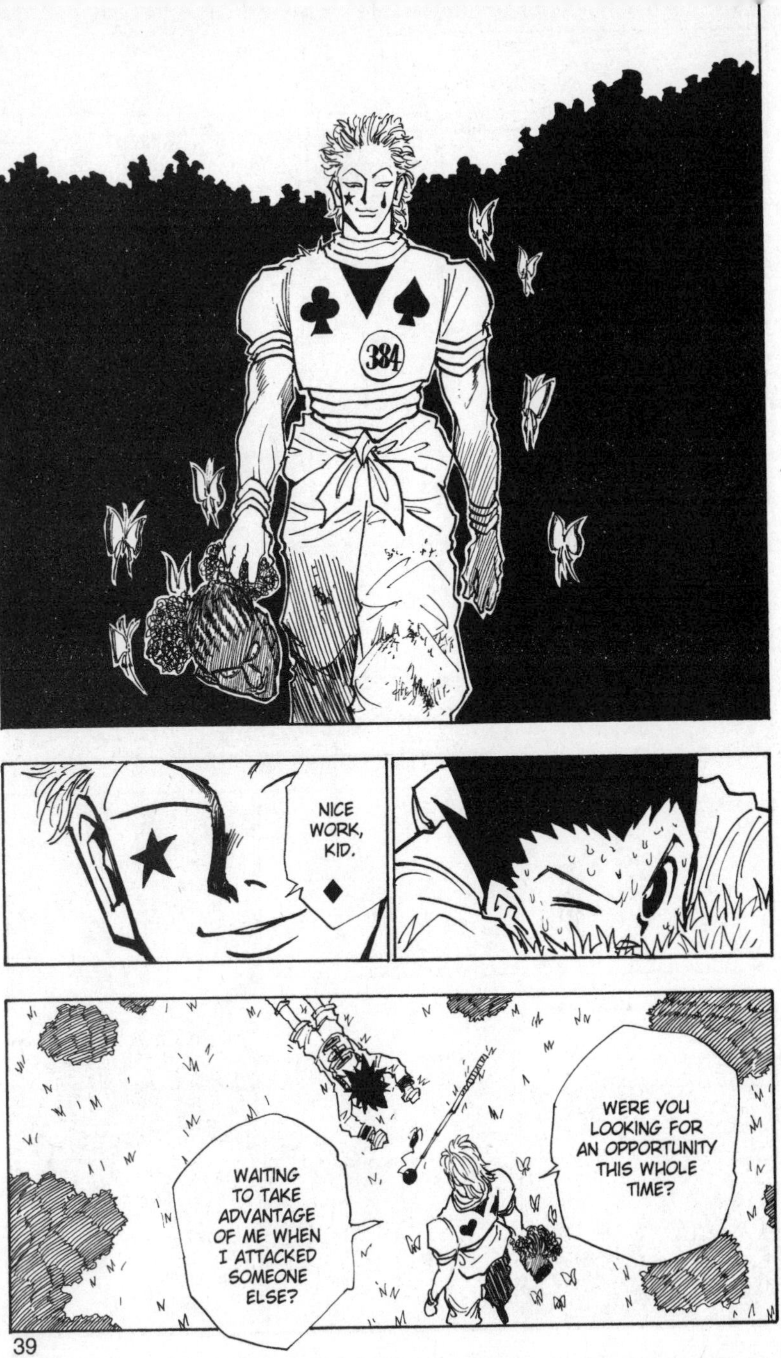

WERE YOU LOOKING FOR AN OPPORTUNITY THIS WHOLE TIME?
WAITING TO TAKE ADVANTAGE OF ME WHEN I ATTACKED SOMEONE ELSE?

YOUR STALKING TECHNIQUE... SELF-TAUGHT?
WHATEVER... IT WAS A ***WORK OF ART***. ♥
PERFECT TIMING...AND MASKING YOUR BLOODLUST...
...BEHIND MINE, SO I DIDN'T DETECT IT RIGHT AWAY. ♣

MASTERFUL. ♥
PLOP

THAT BLOW DART DELIVERED A MUSCLE RELAXANT. ♠
NORMALLY IT TAKES ABOUT ***TEN DAYS*** FOR A FULL RECOVERY. ♣
I'M SURE ***YOU'LL*** BE UP AND ABOUT ***LONG*** BEFORE THEN. ♦
WAIT...
...YOU'RE WALKING OFF...
...WITHOUT YOUR BADGE.
ACTUALLY, I'M ***LEAVING*** IT HERE. ♥

TURNS OUT THIS GUY WAS MY TARGET...
...SO MY BADGE IS... SUPERFLUOUS. ♥
384
TAKE IT ANYWAY.
44
TSK... DON'T BE LIKE THAT. ♠
I DIDN'T RECOVER IT FROM YOU. ♣
SO LET'S JUST SAY YOU OWE ME ONE. ♥
SEE YOU LATER! ♦
♣

GRUURRR...

I'D RATHER OWE YOU NOTHING...

...SO *TAKE* IT--NOW!

44

HEH HEH...

NO.

I CHOOSE NOT TO KILL YOU NOW.

SHUFF

YOU SEE, IT SUITS ME TO LET YOU LIVE UNTIL...

PLORP

...YOU BECOME A TRULY WORTHY OPPONENT. ♠

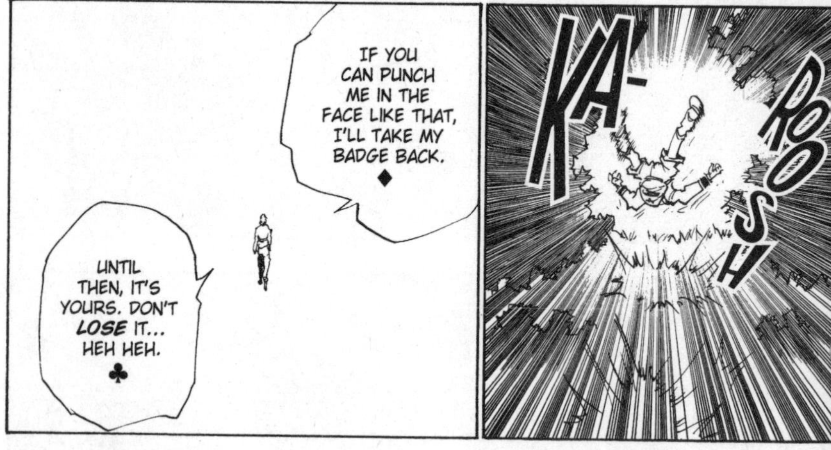
KA-ROOSH
IF YOU CAN PUNCH ME IN THE FACE LIKE THAT, I'LL TAKE MY BADGE BACK. ♦
UNTIL THEN, IT'S YOURS. DON'T *LOSE* IT... HEH HEH. ♣

HEH
HEH
HEH

READ THIS WAY

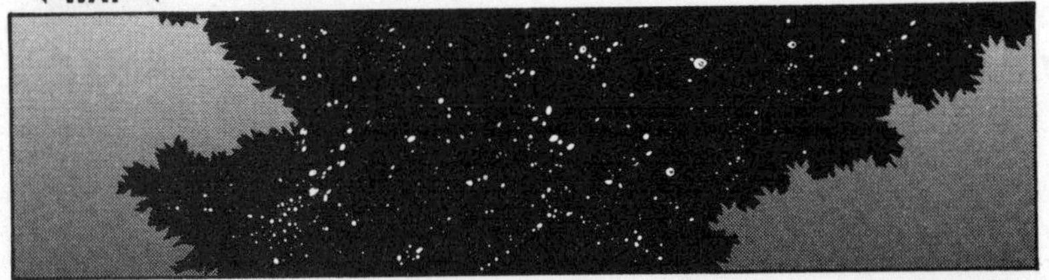

Chapter 29

Killua's Case

YOU'RE JUST WASTING TIME.

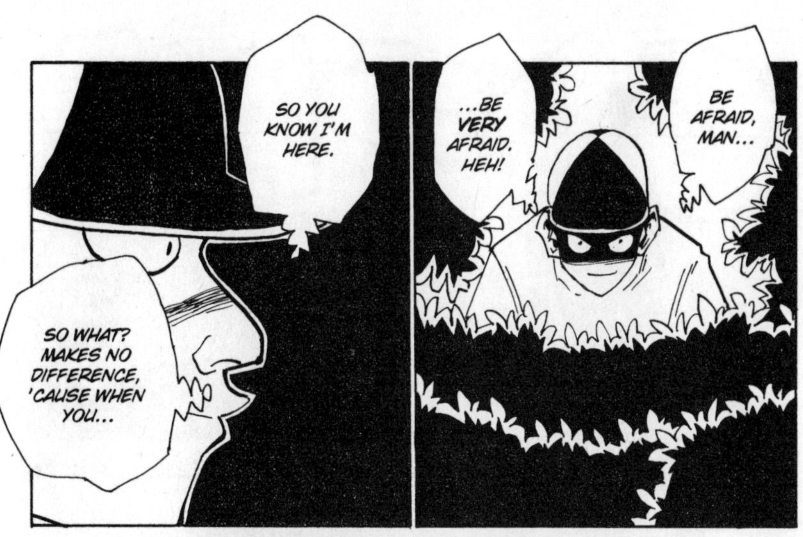
SO YOU KNOW I'M HERE.
SO WHAT? MAKES NO DIFFERENCE, 'CAUSE WHEN YOU...
...BE VERY AFRAID. HEH!
BE AFRAID, MAN...

...I'LL HAVE YOU!
HEH HEH
...FINALLY SUCCUMB TO EXHAUSTION...

BRAVE THOUGHTS, BUT WHAT ABOUT HIS HEART?
YEP...BE AFRAID, KID.
INCH INCH

GASP!!
OH, VERY WELL... HERE I COME.

IT'S ANNOYING, Y'KNOW.
SHUFF
SHUFF
YOU'RE PROBABLY JUST A ONE-POINTER.
BUPPA
BUPPA
BUPPA
BUPPA

NOW WHAT?! SHOULD I ENGAGE?! NO WAY I'D LOSE! HE'S JUST A SNOTNOSE KID!
BUPPA
BUPPA
BUPPA
BUPPA
BUPPA
BUT HE'S NOT AFRAID... SO MAYBE I SHOULD RUN AWAY--I MEAN, RETREAT AND REASSESS!
BUPPA
BUPPA

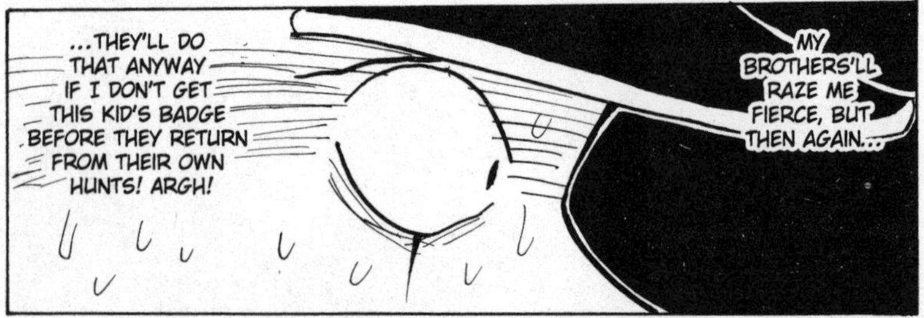
MY BROTHERS'LL RAZE ME FIERCE, BUT THEN AGAIN...
...THEY'LL DO THAT ANYWAY IF I DON'T GET THIS KID'S BADGE BEFORE THEY RETURN FROM THEIR OWN HUNTS! ARGH!

SHUFF
SHUFF
SO HOW'S IT *GOING*, IMORI?
AMORI! UMORI!
?!

SORRY WE TOOK SO LONG.
BUT *YOU'RE* DONE, RIGHT?

EH?

BOOT POW

YOU WUSS!

YOU HAVEN'T TAKEN OUT THAT LITTLE KID YET?!

HEY, I WAS JUST...

THE THRILL'S IN THE CHASE, YEAH?

...I MEAN, WHY RUSH IT?

I'LL THRILL YA...

WHOA! HEY!

GUESS I SHOULD WRAP THIS UP.

HEH HEH

HERE I GO...

...

SHUMF
HAND OVER YER BADGE, KID...
...AN' YOU WON'T GET HURT, RIGHT?
IDIOT.
WHAM

THUD
AWW...
...WOT A WIMP!

SOLAR PLEXUS KICK!
DOWN IN ONE!

...

READ THIS WAY

HIP!
HUP!
TUMP!
AW, Y'JUST WHIFFED 'IM.
YOU'RE TOYIN' WITH 'IM, YEAH?
UM...
... YEAH ...
SUFF
NUMBER 198.

...
198

...

ALMOST, BUT NOT QUITE.
198

I'M AFTER *199.*
THAT EITHER OF *YOU TWO,* BY CHANCE?

WE GOT OURSELVES A ***LIVE ONE.***

TUMP
TUMP
SPRING

WHOA! ABOVE US!!

TAP

...
KEEP STILL.

MY NAILS ARE RAZOR SHARP.

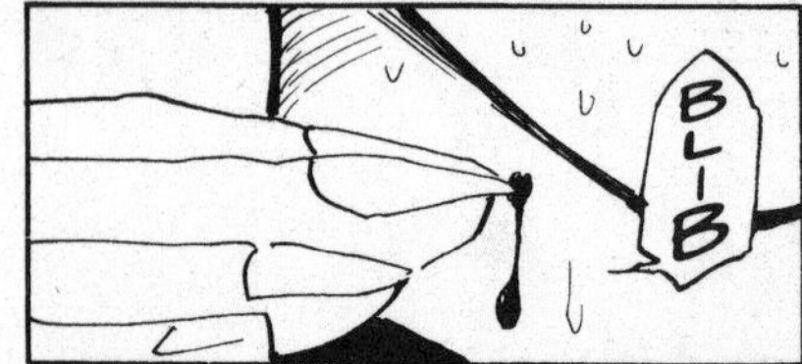
BLIB

NUMBER 197... SHUCKS.
I NEVER WAS ANY GOOD AT GUESSING. OH WELL...

...MAYBE *YOU'RE* 199?

...

YEAH.

GIMME!

FWING
WOOSH!

READ
THIS
WAY

FFT

FWIIING
THERE GOES THE OTHER ONE!

YOU HAVE FIVE DAYS LEFT TO RECOVER THEM. GOOD LUCK.

SEE YA!
SHWUFF
SHWIFF

AARGH!

ZWING
ZWING
ZWING

FWOOOSH
FWIFFT
FWIFFT
FWIFFT
FWISH

SNAP

MY TARGET, 197, ALWAYS STAYED WITH 199...
...SO I WAS STUCK JUST TRACKING HIM, UNTIL...
TOOMP

TWING
...THAT KID WOUND UP SNAGGING HIS BADGE FOR ME. ALL I HAD TO DO...

SNAP!
...WAS CHASE IT! AND NOW, WITH MY BADGE, I'M ALL...

198

Chapter 30

The Slithering Trap

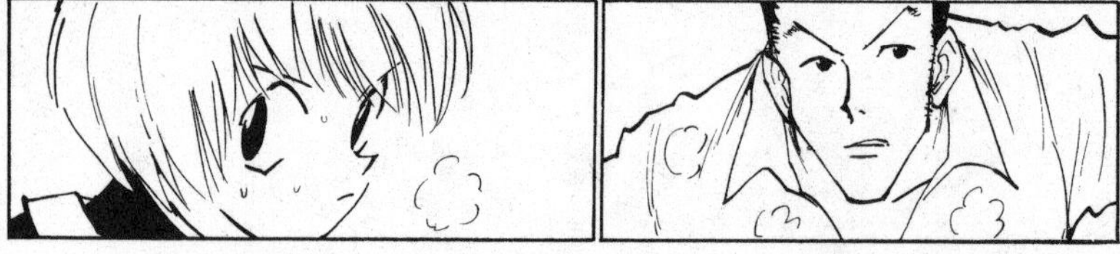

IT'S BEEN ALMOST SIX DAYS.
JUST ONE DAY LEFT.

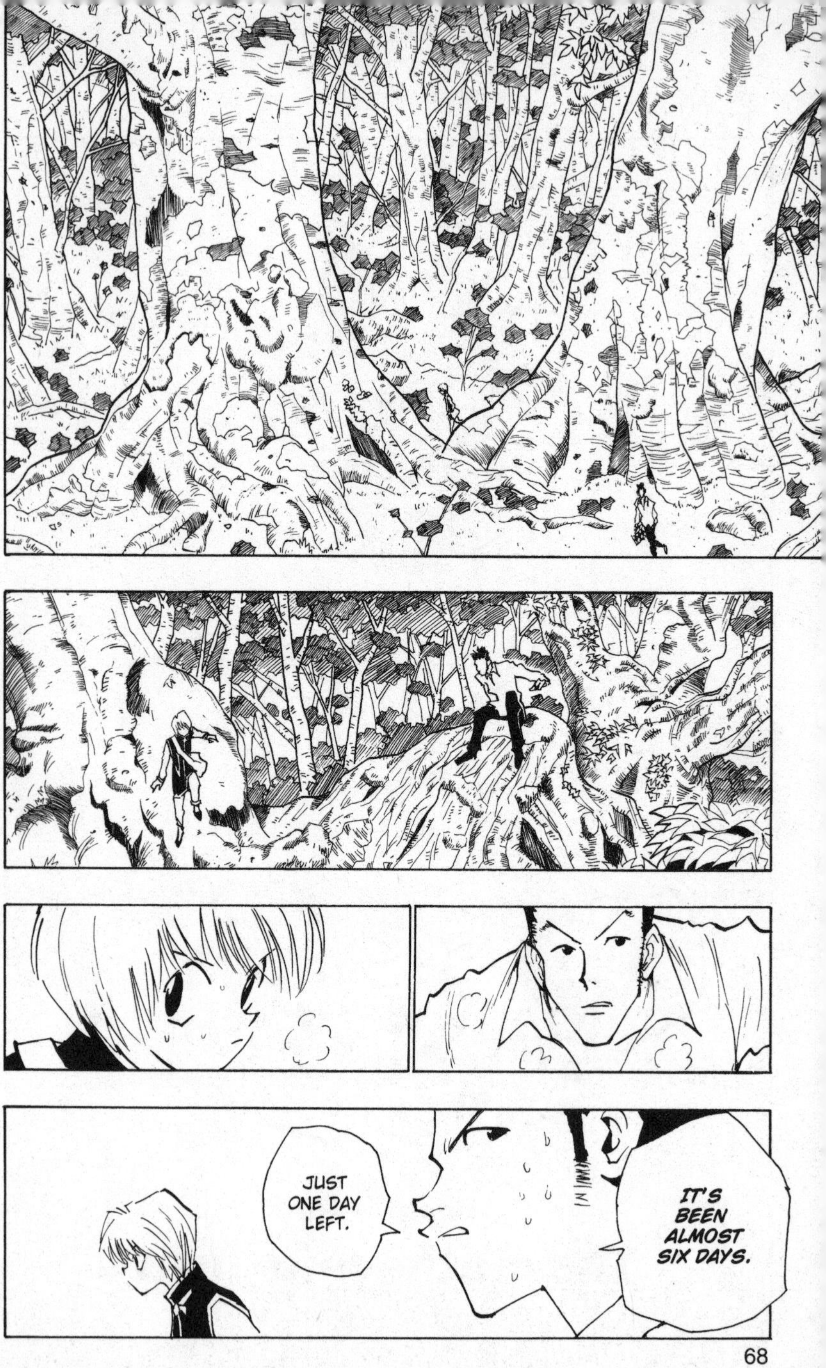

READ THIS WAY

OUR LAST ENCOUNTER WAS WITH HISOKA...
...AND THAT WAS THREE DAYS AGO.
HMM...

MAYBE WE SHOULD GO BACK TO THE LANDING...

...AND SEE IF ANYONE'S ALREADY PASSED.
NO POINT. NO ONE HAS.
THOUGH WE HAVE TO CAPTURE BADGES...
...THAT IS, IN FACT, ONLY ONE PART OF THE CHALLENGE.
EVEN IF YOU GET YOUR SIX POINTS WORTH...
...YOU HAVE TO HOLD ONTO THEM UNTIL TIME IS UP.

AND THAT WON'T BE UNTIL TOMORROW.
OH... RIGHT.

STILL... IT MIGHT BE WORTH CHECKING.
SINCE THERE IS ONLY ONE DAY LEFT...
...THOSE WHO ALREADY HAVE THEIR SIX POINTS...
...WOULD NATURALLY WANT TO MAKE THEIR WAY BACK TO THE FINISH LINE.
I WOULD CERTAINLY DO THAT.
OKAY.
LET'S GO TAKE A LOOK.

SLOOSH

NO SIGN OF ANYONE.
NO...
...BUT THEY WOULD HARDLY BE LOUNGING ON THE BEACH.
HMPH...

I GUESS WE GO BACK TO HUNTING.
WE CAN SET A TIME AND PLACE TO RENDEZVOUS ...
CAN I GET IN ON THIS?

!!

SHOOP
GON!!
THIS SEEMS TO BE A POPULAR PLACE.
I SPOTTED SEVERAL OTHER EXAMINEES HANGING AROUND.
FROM *UP THERE*?
WHY DIDN'T *WE* THINK OF THAT?
TO WHAT *PURPOSE?* IT REQUIRED GON'S EYESIGHT.
DO YOU HAVE *YOUR* BADGES, GON?

YEAH... I HAVE 'EM.
SHOOT! *I'M* THE ONLY ONE LEFT!
I NEED TO FIND 246--A WOMAN NAMED PONZU.
YOU DIDN'T HAPPEN TO SPOT *HER*, DID YOU?

'FRAID NOT.
RATS! OH WELL...
LET'S CONSIDER THE PROSPECTS ...
ONE. SHE'S ALIVE AND STILL HAS HER BADGE.
TWO. SHE'S ALIVE, BUT SHE'S LOST HER BADGE.
THREE. SHE'S DEAD, BUT SHE STILL HAS HER BADGE.
FOUR. SHE'S DEAD, AND SHE'S LOST HER BADGE.

WHOA! THREE MAKES NO SENSE! HOW COULD SHE HAVE HER BADGE IF SHE'S DEAD?
SHE MAY HAVE HAD AN ACCIDENT, OR WAS ATTACKED ONLY AFTER SHE HAD HIDDEN HER BADGE SOMEWHERE.

IF THE LATTER, AND SHE WAS SLAIN IN THE ATTACK...
...THAT BADGE MIGHT NEVER BE FOUND.
GRR ...
...THIS IS LOOKING HOPELESS... FOR ME, ANYWAY.

DOES SHE HAVE ANY PARTICULAR TRAITS?
SAY, WEARING A FRAGRANCE LIKE LEORIO?
?
HMM ...

READ THIS WAY

...THAT IS A THOUGHT! GON MIGHT BE ABLE TO TRACK HER BY SMELL!
BUT HOW DO WE KNOW SHE'S WEARING A FRAGRANCE?

IT MAY BE A GIVEN!
SHE USES CHEMICAL WEAPONS, RIGHT?
SOME OF THEM SURELY HAVE DISTINCTIVE ODORS.

WHAT ABOUT IT, GON?
WORTH A SHOT!

I CAME TO HELP, Y'KNOW.
?
...

!
THIS WAY...
...WE'RE CLOSE!
SHEOOOO
SHUFF

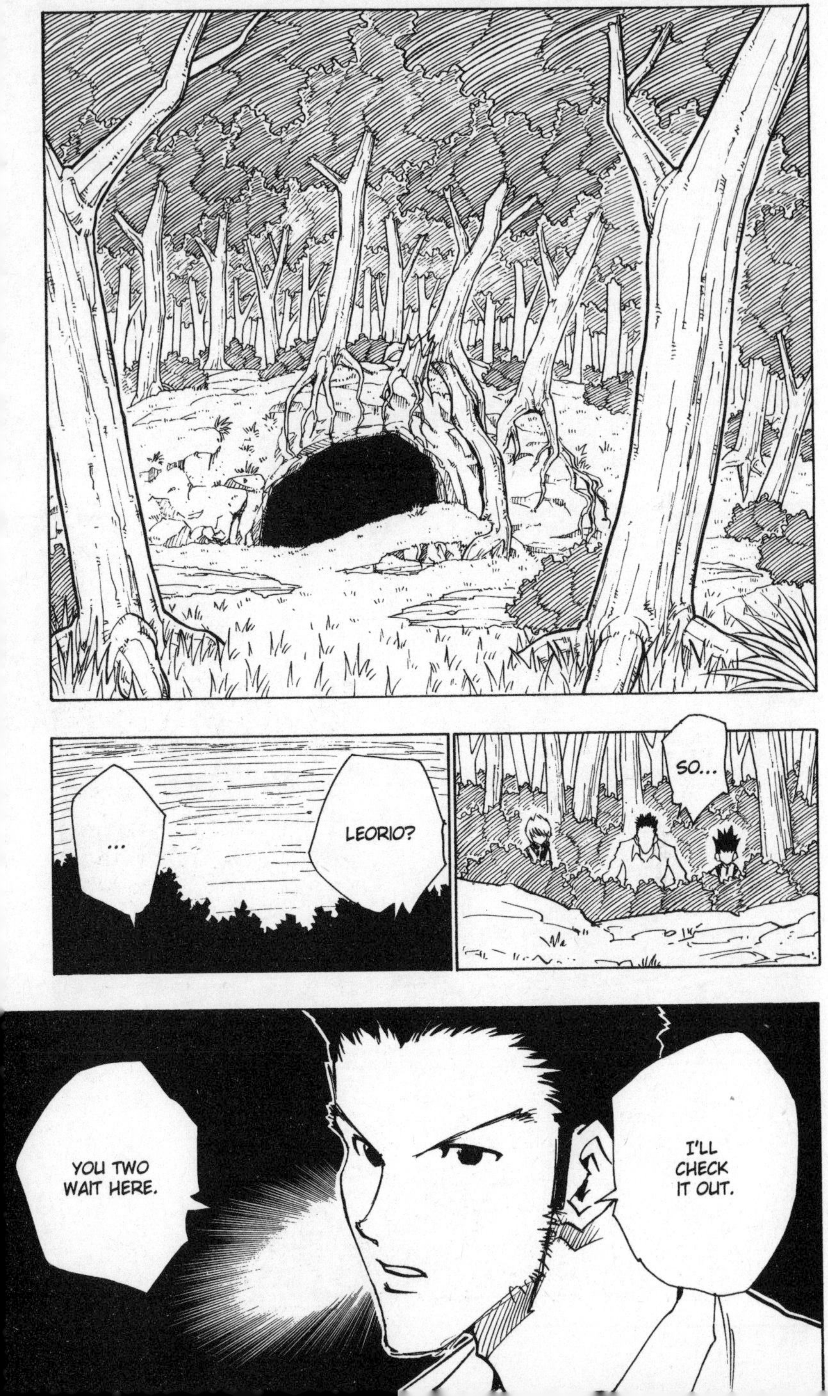

SO...
LEORIO?
...

I'LL CHECK IT OUT.
YOU TWO WAIT HERE.

SHUFF

TAP TAP

SEEMS CLEAR OF TRAPS.

I'D BETTER GO INSIDE.
STAY PUT, UNTIL I GIVE THE "ALL CLEAR."
WE WILL WAIT 30 MINUTES...
...IF WE DON'T HEAR FROM YOU BY THEN...
...NO MATTER WHAT, WE FOLLOW.

NO!!
JUST FORGET ME! GET BACK TO THE LANDING!
THAT IS NOT AN OPTION...

...IN AN ALLIANCE ...
WE WON'T LEAVE YOU BEHIND.

THEN THE ALLIANCE IS OVER!!
THANKS FOR YOUR HELP, BUT FROM HERE ON OUT...
...THIS IS MY SHOW!
NUH-UH.
NO.
WHAT?!

WE'RE **STAYING**, SIMPLE AS THAT!

WANNA **MAKE** SOMETHING OF IT?

READ THIS WAY

PEEP
CHEEP

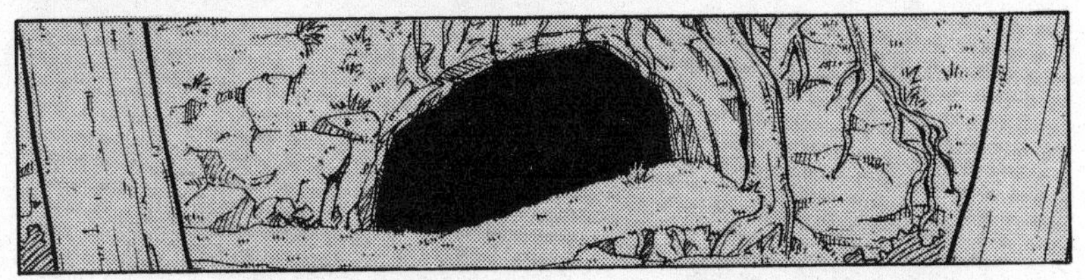

...

GON!! KURAPIKA!! STAY BACK!!

SNAKES !!

!!

LEORIO
!!

SLITHER
SLITHER
SLITHER

SLITHER
SLITHER

TRUP
TRUP
TRUP
TRUP

!!

TWITCH
TWITCH
LEORIO!

READ
THIS
WAY

YOU... IDIOTS...
TOLDJA... T' SCRAM ...!

HE'S COVERED IN BITES!!
IF THESE ARE VIPERS...

FIP

THEY'RE VIPERS, ALL RIGHT! NOT ALL THAT VENOMOUS, BUT...
...HE'S BEEN BITTEN ENOUGH TO GET A FATAL DOSE!

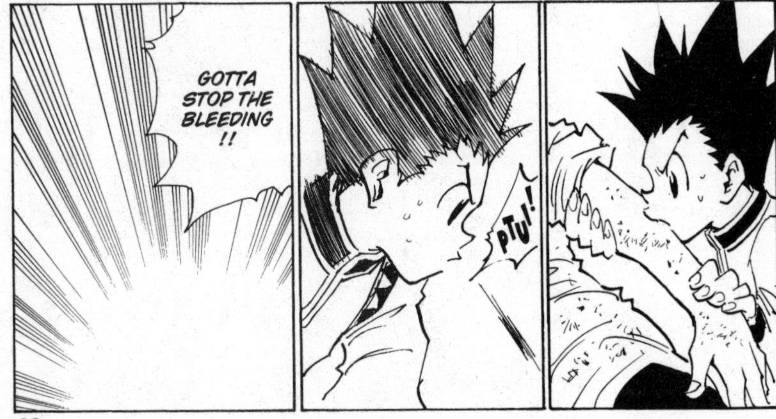
PTU!
GOTTA STOP THE BLEEDING !!

HE NEEDS A DOCTOR! COME ON!
I WOULDN'T ADVISE IT.
YOU'RE TRAPPED IN HERE.
!!

IF YOU TRY TO LEAVE THIS CAVE...
...THE SNAKES WILL ATTACK YOU EN MASSE!

HISS
HISS
HISS
HISS
!!
BOURBON, THE SNAKE CHARMER, SET THIS UP...

SLITHER
HISS
SLITHER
LIKE YOUR FRIEND THERE...
...YOU'LL BE ***PARALYZED***, THEN YOU'LL ***SLOWLY DIE.***

Chapter 31
By the Skin of Their Teeth...

DEAD...?
SLITHER
SLITHER
SLITHER
SLITHER
HIISSS
HIISSS

READ THIS WAY

HE SET THIS TRAP, YET HE IS DEAD?
HOW?!

I KILLED HIM.
"HOW" IS MY BUSINESS.

GON, TAKE LEORIO.
SURE.

SUH

!!
SLITHER
SLITHER
SLITHER
SLITHER
SLITHER
SLITHER

HIISSS
HIISSS
HSSSSST

READ THIS WAY

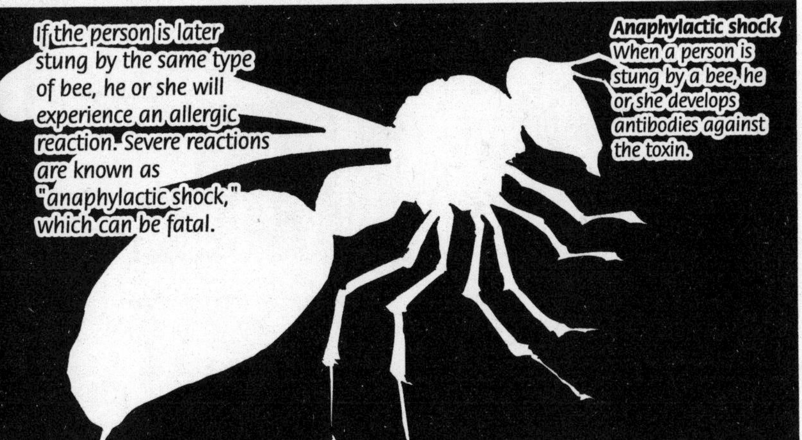

WHILE STALKING HIM, I SAW HIM ENTER THIS CAVE...
...SO I SHOT SLEEPING GAS THROUGH THE ENTRANCE...
...LET IT TAKE EFFECT, THEN WENT INSIDE.

Y'SEE, IF I'M STARTLED OR JERKED ABOUT...

...THESE LITTLE GUYS POP OUT AND GO TO IT.

POP

POP

KILLING HIM WASN'T THE **IDEA**, OF COURSE.

BUT HOW WAS I TO KNOW HE WAS **ALLERGIC?**

ADMINISTERING FIRST AID WAS OUT OF THE QUESTION.

HISSSS

HISSSS

HE DIED, AND THERE WAS **NOTHING** I COULD DO.

WORSE, HIS DEATH **HASN'T DEACTIVATED HIS TRAP.**

IT'S OKAY... GO BACK NOW.

SEEMS THESE SNAKES WILL **PROTECT** THEIR MASTER...

...FOR AS LONG AS THEY'RE **ALIVE** TO DO HIM **THAT SERVICE.**

WHICH MEANS WE'RE **STUCK.**

THE COMMITTEE ONLY ATTEMPTS RESCUES...

...ONCE A PHASE IS ***OVER.*** UNTIL THEN, THE EXAMINEES ARE ON THEIR OWN.

REMEMBER, THIS IS THE SAME COMMITTEE THAT LETS EXAMINEES ***MURDER*** EACH OTHER.

ANYWAY, IT'S ON HIS HEAD. I ***WARNED*** HIM...

...BUT HE ***IGNORED ME*** AND RAN UP TO THE EXIT—

GON!! KURAPIKA!! STAY BACK!

SNAKES!

YOU'LL HAVE TO HOPE...
...HE'LL BE ABLE TO LAST UNTIL HELP ARRIVES.
NO... THERE IS...
...SOMETHING WE CAN TRY!
BUT IF WE ARE WRONG, THE SNAKES...
...WILL CLAIM ANOTHER VICTIM!!

...
KURAPIKA, YOU TAKE LEORIO...

I'LL MAKE THIS PLAY!!

SHUFF
SHUFF

WHAT'RE YOU DOING?!
ARE YOU CRAZY?!

GLOM

!!
CHOMP!!
CHOMP!!

DAMN...
...HE WENT RIGHT IN...

HISSS
HISSSS
GROPE
PLUP
HISS
HISSS
PLOP
GROPE

FOUND IT!!

TOSS
CATCH!!
SNAP
THUMP!!
GON, YOU--
GIVE IT TO... LEORIO FIRST...

HE WAS... LOOKING FOR AN ANTIDOTE?!
YOU COULDN'T KNOW HE HAD ONE!
SIGH...
IT WAS QUITE LIKELY, THOUGH.
POISON IS A POOR NEGOTIATING TOOL WITHOUT AN ANTIDOTE.
OW!
Honestly ...
STILL, IT TAKES A LOT OF COURAGE TO THROW ONESELF INTO A THRONG OF SNAKES LIKE THAT.

SAY...
Phew...
...YOU HAVE ANY OF THAT SLEEPING GAS LEFT?

...?
SOME. WHY?
!!
I'LL TRADE THAT FOR THIS!
103
IT'LL GIVE YOU SIX POINTS, RIGHT?

SLITHER

SLITHER

RELEASING THE GAS IN HERE **WOULD** BE MUCH MORE EFFECTIVE THAN WHEN I DID IT FROM THE ENTRANCE.

SLITHE

SLITHER

THE GAS WILL PERMEATE THE CAVE, GETTING INTO EVERY CREVICE AND PUTTING ALL THE SNAKES TO SLEEP.

READ THIS WAY

PLOP
PLUP
FSSH
FSSH
201...
202...
...

FSSSH
SHUFF
FSSSH

AH
TA-DA
WHOO-EEE!!
HAAAH!!

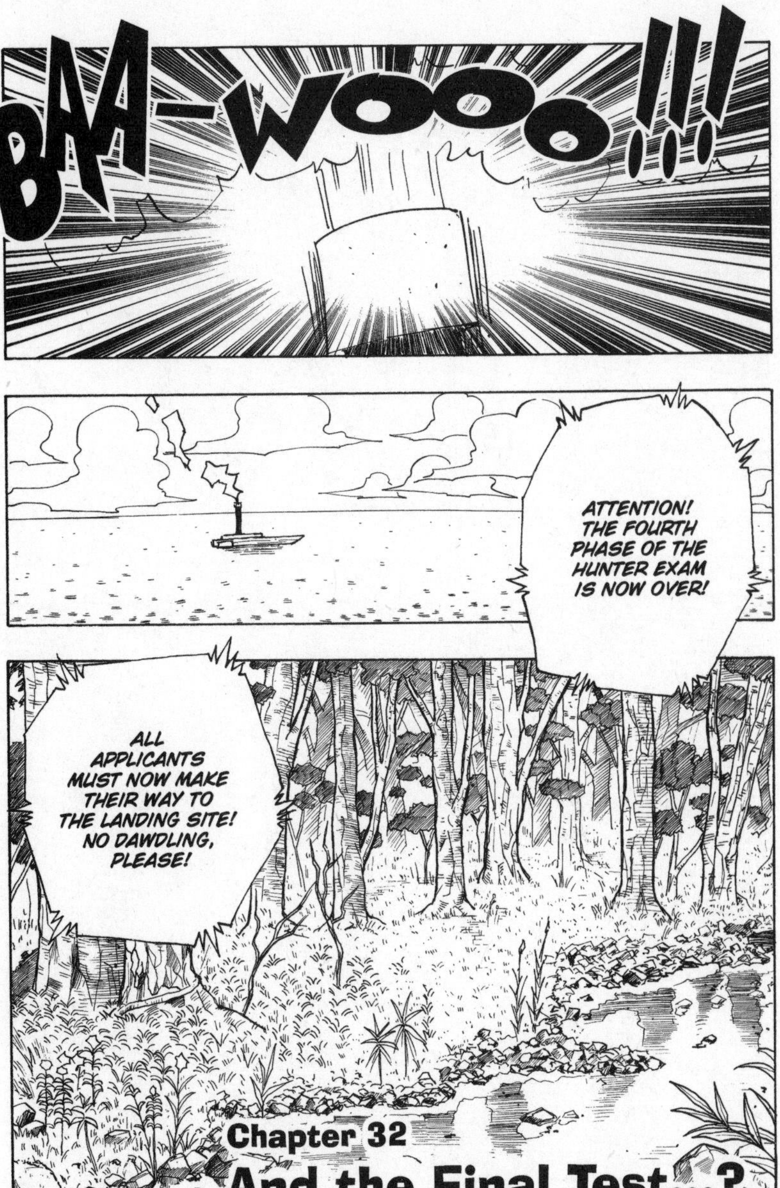

ATTENTION! THE FOURTH PHASE OF THE HUNTER EXAM IS NOW OVER!

ALL APPLICANTS MUST NOW MAKE THEIR WAY TO THE LANDING SITE! NO DAWDLING, PLEASE!

Chapter 32
And the Final Test...?

YOU HAVE ONE HOUR TO SHOW UP! ONE HOUR ONLY!
ANYONE NOT AT THE LANDING SITE BY THEN WILL BE FAILED!
SHUSS
RUSTLE

ONCE AT THE LANDING SITE, YOU ARE NEITHER HUNTER NOR TARGET!
TRUDGE
TRUDGE
ANY ATTEMPT TO TRANSFER BADGES AT THIS POINT WILL RESULT IN IMMEDIATE DISQUALIFIC-ATION!

BADGES
384(3)
80(1)
281(1)
118(1)
405(3)
44(3)
404(3)
16(3)
53(3)
105(3)
403(3)
246(3)
301(3)
371(3)
99(3)
199(3)
191(3)
34(3)
294(3)
198(1)
362(1)
89(1)

Chapter 32
And the Final Test...?

RRMMM

WHIRR

WHIRR

WELL NOW, **SIX OUT OF NINE** ARE **ROOKIES!**

QUITE A **SHOWING** BY THE **NEW BLOOD** THIS YEAR!

HAS THAT EVER HAPPENED?

SURE...

...THOUGH IT USUALLY FOLLOWS A PATTERN.

A DECADE GOES BY, THERE'RE NO ROOKIES WORTH BEANS...

...THEN ONE YEAR A WHOLE **GAGGLE** OF 'EM SHOW UP AND **BEAT THE PANTS OFF** THE **VETS!**

THIS MAKES **FOUR TIMES** SINCE *I* BECAME CHAIRMAN.
REALLY? WOW!
WHIRR
WHIRR
HOW *OLD* IS HE ANYWAY?
ABOUT A 100, HE SAYS... THOUGH HE'S BEEN SAYING THAT FOR 20 YEARS.
ANYONE KNOW THE ***SET UP*** FOR THE ***FINAL PHASE?***
CHOMP

READ
THIS
WAY

TO PREPARE, I'D LIKE...
...TO HAVE A WORD WITH *EACH* OF THE NINE.

WHAT COULD *THAT* MEAN?
BEATS ME!
BUT WE'D BEST *BRACE* OURSELVES!

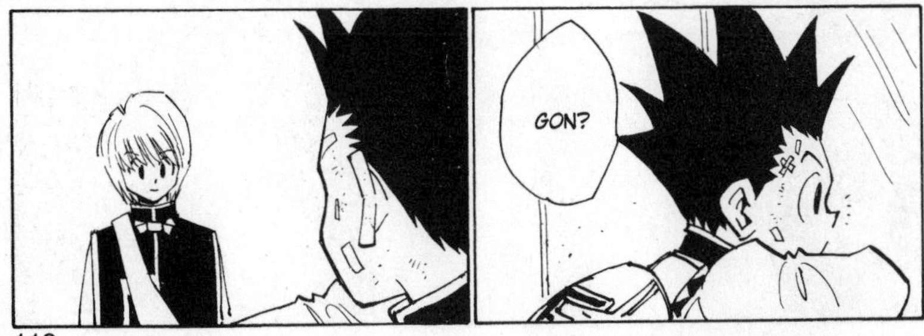
GON?

THE FINAL PHASE LIES AHEAD.
YEAH ...
YOU ENABLED ME TO GET THIS FAR.
ME? NOT HARDLY!

GON...
HMM...?

ARE YOU ALL RIGHT? DID SOMETHING... HAPPEN?
YOU HAVE BEEN SOMEWHAT DISTRACTED...
...SINCE WE MET UP AGAIN.
...

READ THIS WAY

I...DREW HISOKA.
!

STILL, I MANAGED TO GET HIS BADGE.
BUT I WASN'T WATCHING MY BACK, AND SOMEONE ELSE...
...GOT ME WITH A BLOW DART. BING... BADGE GONE!

HISOKA NAILED THE OTHER GUY AND...
...RETURNED HIS BADGE TO ME...A FAVOR, HE SAID.

I TOLD HIM NO THANKS, SO HE CLOBBERED ME!
HE SAID HE'D TAKE BACK HIS BADGE ONLY IF I MANAGE TO CLOBBER HIM.
THAT'S HOW IT WENT DOWN, WITH ME...
...FEELING VERY FRUSTRATED!

RUB RUB
FUNNY, I...DIDN'T WANNA BE ALONE AFTER THAT!
I JUST FELT INADEQUATE ALL BY MYSELF.

READ THIS WAY

I GUESS I CRAVED...WELL, SUPPORT...
...AND A WAY TO MAKE MYSELF FEEL WORTHWHILE...

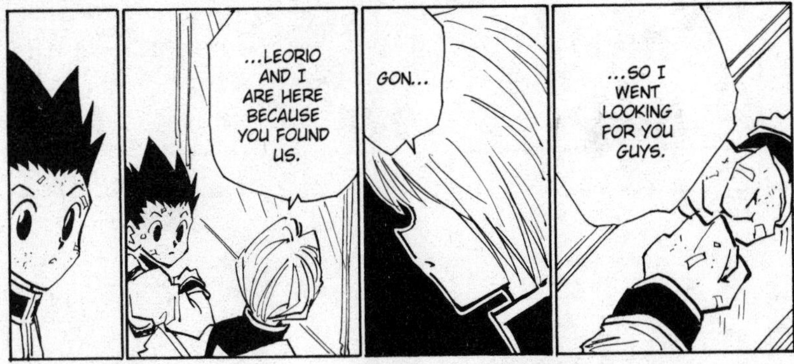
...SO I WENT LOOKING FOR YOU GUYS.
GON...
...LEORIO AND I ARE HERE BECAUSE YOU FOUND US.

YOU ARE ANYTHING BUT INADEQUATE.

GOSH, KURAPIKA, THANKS...
...THANKS A LOT.

ATTENTION! THE CHAIRMAN IS NOW CONDUCTING INTERVIEWS!
PLEASE REPORT TO THE RECEPTION ROOM, DECK TWO WHEN YOUR NUMBER IS CALLED.
RRRM
RRRM
FIRST, NUMBER 44!
NUMBER 44, PLEASE!

INTERVIEWS ...?

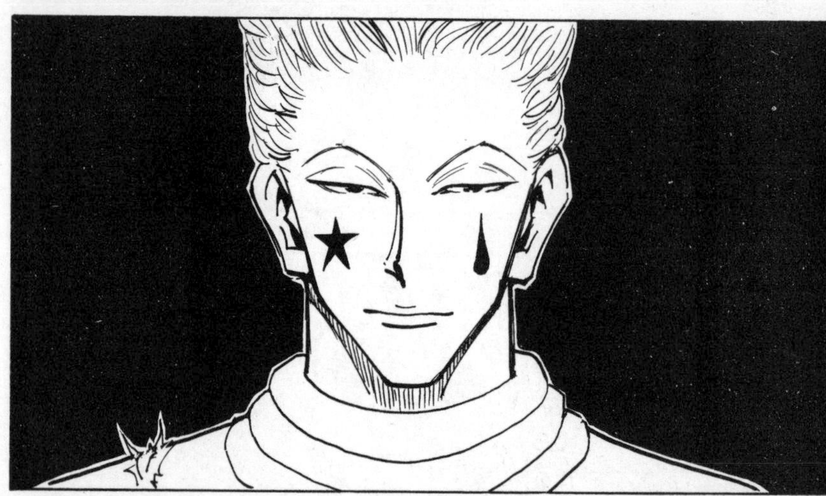

READ THIS WAY

AH YES... HAVE A SEAT.

DON'T TELL ME THIS IS THE FINAL TEST?!
NOT THE TEST ITSELF, NO. I JUST...
...WANT TO ASK A COUPLE QUESTIONS BEFOREHAND.

SO... WHY DO YOU WANT TO BE A HUNTER?
I DON'T AS SUCH, BUT...
...THE LICENSE DOES HAVE ITS USES. ♥

FOR INSTANCE, YOU CAN KILL...
...AND, MORE OFTEN THAN NOT, ESCAPE THE CONSEQUENCES. ♠

ALL RIGHT.
WHO INTERESTS YOU MOST OF THE EIGHT REMAINING EXAMINEES?
NUMBER 99. ♥

I'D LIKE TO CHALLENGE 99 SOMETIME. ♦
THOUGH 405 ALSO CAUGHT MY EYE. ♣

HEH HEH HEH. ♥
I SEE. ONE LAST QUESTION...
...WHOM WOULD YOU LEAST LIKE TO FIGHT RIGHT NOW?
...

I WOULD SAY...405. ♣
...I FEEL THE SAME FOR 99, BUT...

...THE TIME SIMPLY ISN'T RIGHT...
...TO FIGHT 405 YET. ♦
FOR THE RECORD, I'D VERY MUCH...
...LIKE TO FIGHT ***YOU*** RIGHT NOW. ♠

OKAY, THANK YOU.
Hmm...
THAT WILL BE ALL.
...

SLAM
THAT'S ONE SLY OLD FOX. ♠
MY MALEVOLENCE COULDN'T MATCH HIS IN-DIFFERENCE. ♣

TO MY EYE, 404 SEEMS THE MOST WELL-ROUNDED.
I'D AVOID 44, THOUGH... WOULDN'T STAND A *CHANCE* AGAINST HIM.

I GUESS GON... I MEAN, 405. HE'S *MY AGE*, TOO.
53 HARDLY SEEMS WORTH THE TIME OR EFFORT TO ME.

THAT WOULD BE 44. YOU CAN'T *HELP* BUT NOTICE HIM.
405 AND 99 ARE OUT. I WILL NOT FIGHT CHILDREN.

NUMBER 99.
NUMBER 44.

READ THIS WAY

HISOKA, 44, IS CERTAINLY THE ONE MOST ON MY MIND.
AND I'D HATE TO TANGLE WITH EITHER 99, 403, OR 404.

NUMBER 44. HE'S THE MOST CHALLENGING.
NUMBER 44. HE'S THE MOST DANGEROUS.

405 IN A POSITIVE WAY... 44 IN A NEGATIVE WAY.
I FIGHT IF THERE IS A REASON, OTHERWISE I DO NOT. PERSONALITY IS NOT A FACTOR.

NUMBER 405. HE'S QUITE AMAZING IN HIS WAY, AND FRANKLY, I OWE HIM.
THOSE ARE THE SAME REASONS WHY I WOULDN'T WANT TO FIGHT HIM.

WELL, WELL...
...THAT SHOULD SET THINGS UP ABOUT RIGHT.

FWIK
DONE AND DONE!
OKAY, EVERYONE ...
...I'VE GOT THE MATCHUPS.

MR. CHAIRMAN, SIR...
...ARE YOU SERIOUS?

READ THIS WAY

QUITE SERIOUS.
THAT LOOK... HE MEANS IT!
HEH HEH

THANK YOU, EVERYONE! WE APPRECIATE YOUR PATIENCE!
NOW RELAX WHILE WE TRAVEL TO THE SITE OF THE FINALS!

WE WISH YOU SUCCESS...
...IN REACHING THE RANKS OF THE HUNTERS.

RRMMM
RRMMM

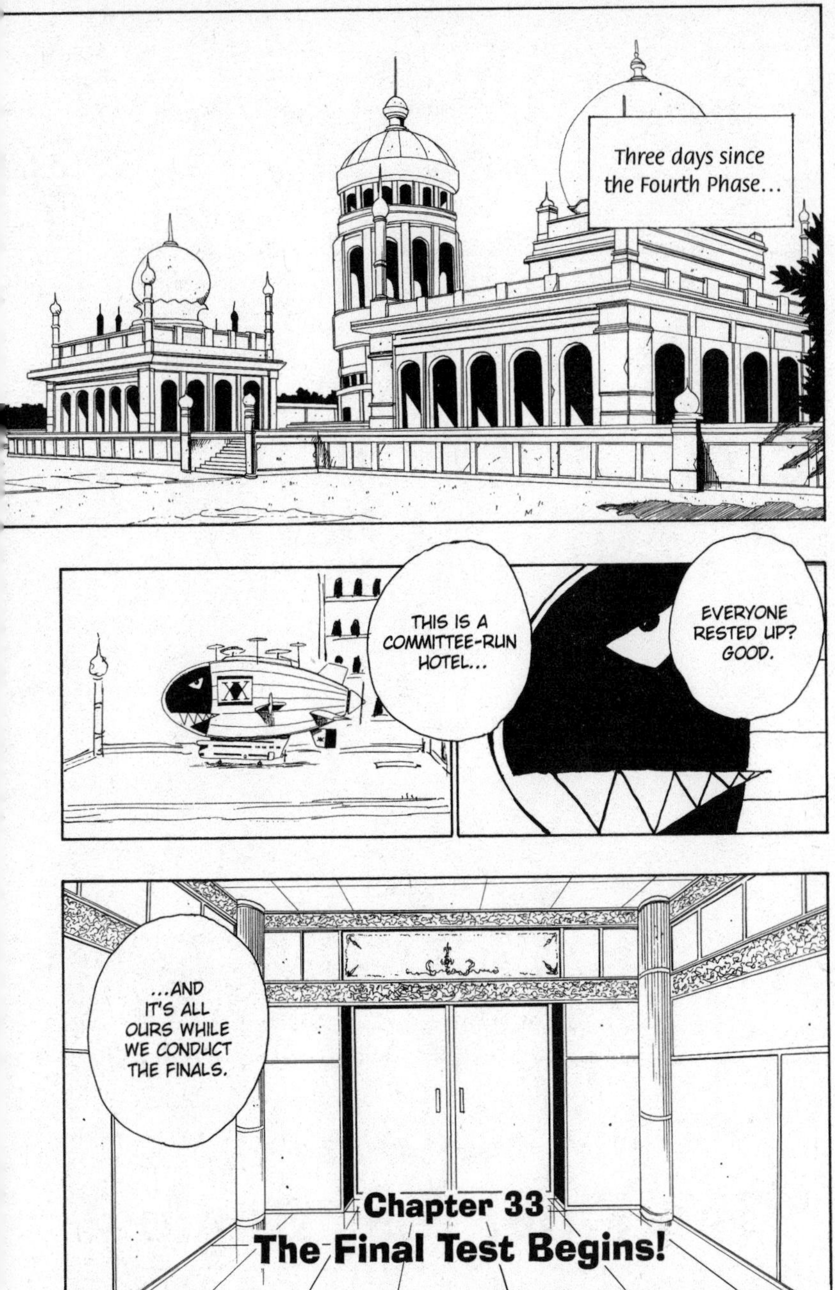

Three days since the Fourth Phase...

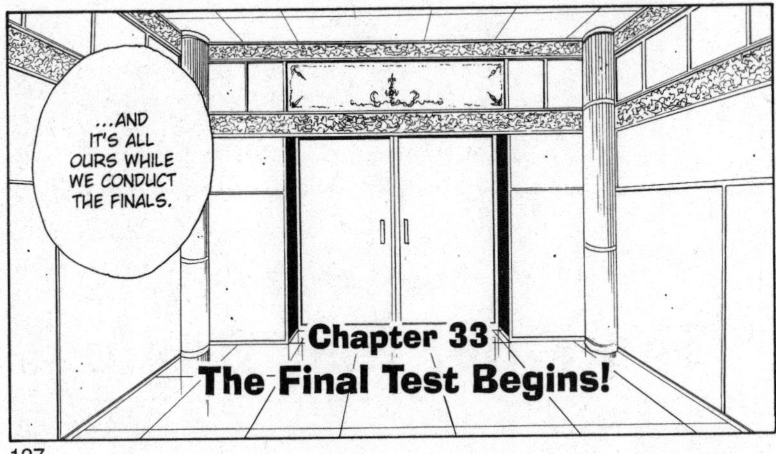

Chapter 33
The Final Test Begins!

Chapter 33

The Final Test Begins!

294 405 53 99 301 191 404 44 403

...

THIS MIGHT LOOK DAUNTING...
...BUT HERE'S THE THING...

BWOOOONG!!
...YOU ONLY NEED ONE WIN TO PASS!!

YOU MEAN ...

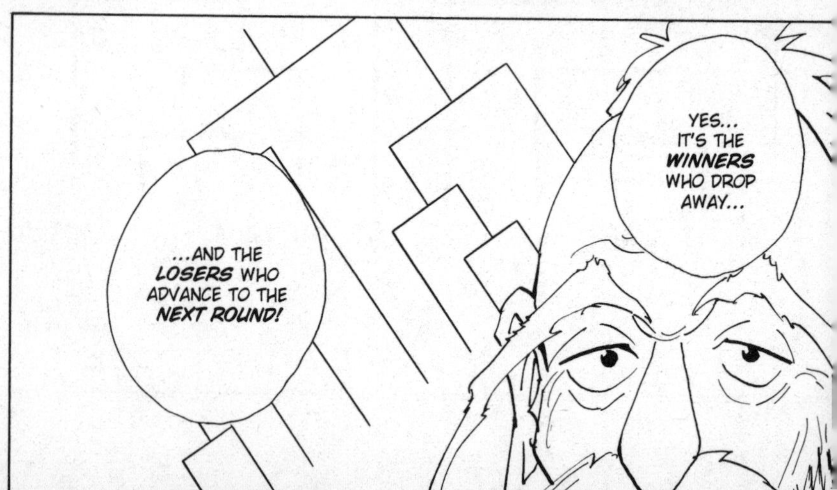
YES... IT'S THE WINNERS WHO DROP AWAY...
...AND THE LOSERS WHO ADVANCE TO THE NEXT ROUND!

THE FINAL ROUND WILL LEAVE ONE WINNER AND ONE LOSER.
HAVE YOU CAUGHT THE DRIFT YET?
ONLY ONE OF US WON'T PASS?
THAT'S RIGHT.
AND YOU EACH HAVE MORE THAN TWO SHOTS AT WINNING.
ANY QUESTIONS?

WHY ARE THE ROUNDS SO OFF-BALANCE?
Love this guy's fashion sense!
AH, NOW THAT'S A FAIR QUESTION.

IT SIMPLY REFLECTS THE EXAM RECORD OF EACH CONTENDER.
IN A NUTSHELL, THOSE WITH THE BEST SCORES GET THE MOST CHANCES TO WIN.

HMPH!
I'M NOT CONVINCED.
WHAT ELSE IS INVOLVED?

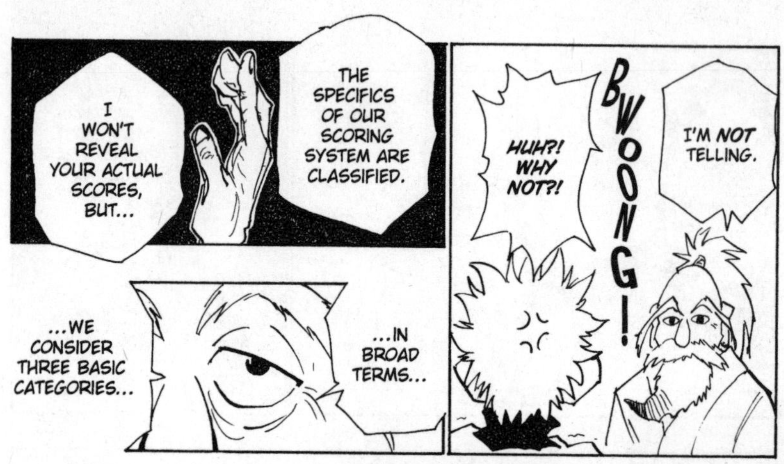
I'M *NOT* TELLING.
HUH?! WHY NOT?!
BWOONG!
THE SPECIFICS OF OUR SCORING SYSTEM ARE CLASSIFIED.
I WON'T REVEAL YOUR ACTUAL SCORES, BUT...
...IN BROAD TERMS...
...WE CONSIDER THREE BASIC CATEGORIES...

...PHYSICAL ABILITY, MENTAL ACUITY...
...AND OVERALL IMPRESSION.

PHYSICAL ABILITY INVOLVES STRENGTH, AGILITY, ENDURANCE, AND THE SENSES.
MENTAL ACUITY IS THE MEASURE OF FOCUS, FLEXIBILITY, JUDGMENT, AND CREATIVITY.
YOU'VE *ALL* REACHED THE FINALS...
...SO THERE'S LITTLE YOU NEED TO PROVE IN THOSE AREAS.
WHAT WE COME TO NOW IS *IMPRES-SION!*

I KNOW I'VE SCORED BETTER THAN GON OVERALL...

...YET THEY SEE MORE POTENTIAL IN HIM?!

THERE ARE JUST A FEW SIMPLE RULES.

YOU MAY USE ANY ***WEAPONS*** YOU LIKE. YOU ***WIN*** WHEN YOUR OPPONENT ***ADMITS DEFEAT!***

HOWEVER...

...IF YOU KILL YOUR OPPONENT, YOU WILL BE DISQUALIFIED!
AT THAT POINT THE EXAM ENDS, YOU FAIL, AND EVERYONE ELSE PASSES!
LET THE FINAL PHASE BEGIN!!
FIRST MATCH—
—HANZO VS. GON!

READ
THIS
WAY

I AM MASTA... I WILL SERVE AS REFEREE...
...AND WIT-NESS.
WE MEET AT LAST!
DID YOU ENJOY MY FOURTH PHASE ADVENTURES?
!

SO YOU KNEW?
SURE DID.

EXAMINERS FOLLOWED EACH APPLICANT DURING THE FOURTH PHASE.
YOU WEREN'T HARD TO MISS. BET OTHERS NOTICED, TOO.

...
Sheesh... I didn't!

I THOUGHT YOU KNEW...

CONSIDERING MY RANK IN THE FINAL, I CLEARLY IMPRESSED YOU TO NO END!
OH-KAY ...
Naturally...
WHOA! POINT OF ORDER!
SNAP
BWOONG
YES?
WHAT A CHATTER-BOX!
ONE'S OPPONENT HAS TO ADMIT DEFEAT, RIGHT?
THERE'S NO WIN IF HE WON'T— OR CAN'T— DO THAT?
THEM'S THE RULES.
HMM...
GLANCE
...SO THAT'S THE CATCH.
BET HE'S NO PUSHOVER... BUT NEITHER AM I!
I'LL DODGE AROUND, CONFUSE HIM, LOOK FOR AN OPENING!
ALL RIGHT...
SHNK
BEGIN !!

DASH
!!

FWIT

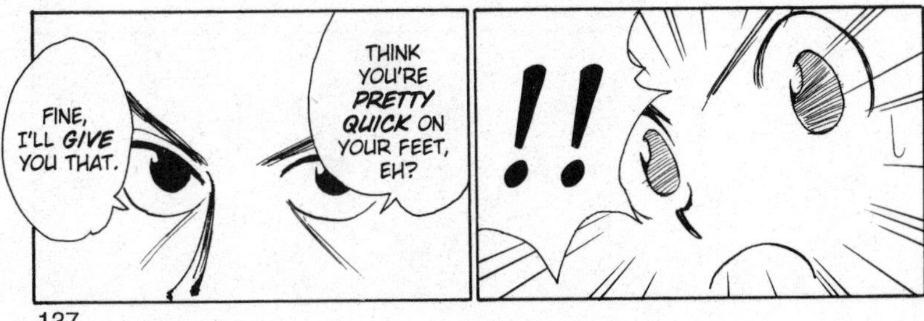
!!
THINK YOU'RE ***PRETTY QUICK*** ON YOUR FEET, EH?
FINE, I'LL ***GIVE*** YOU THAT.

TWACK

NOT BAD...
FOR A KID.

THUD

READ THIS WAY

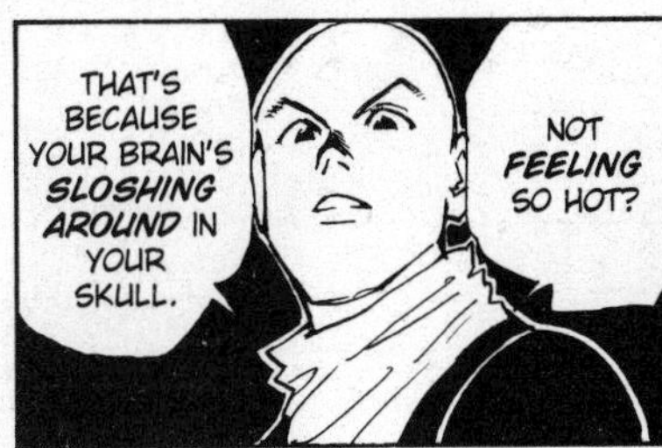

SLOSH
...!!

WHAP

KOFF!

HACK!
STOP NOW, AND YOU'LL HAVE A CHANCE IN THE *NEXT* MATCH.
KOFF!
STUBBORNNESS WILL ONLY *REDUCE* THAT CHANCE.

SO SAY YOU'RE BEATEN.
...!
NO! NEVER!!

WHUMP
UNH!
...

GON, HE'S NOT FOOLING AROUND! YOU SHOULD SAY...
LEORIO!
IF THAT WERE YOU, WOULD YOU GIVE UP?
TO THAT ARROGANT BLOWHARD?! NO FLIPPIN' WAY!!
BUT IT'S NOT ME OUT THERE, IT'S GON!!
STRANGE, THAT IS... JUST HOW I FEEL.

Surrender, Gon!!
Persisting is suicide!!

NEVER SUSPECTED THE CHAIRMAN HAD SUCH A MEAN STREAK.
NO ONE IN THIS FINAL GROUP'S GOING TO THROW IN THE TOWEL WITHOUT TAKING A LOT OF PUNISHMENT!
THIS ISN'T JUST A DIFFERENT WRINKLE—IT'S COMPLETELY TURNED THE THING INSIDE OUT!!
THAT POOR KID'S REALLY IN FOR IT.

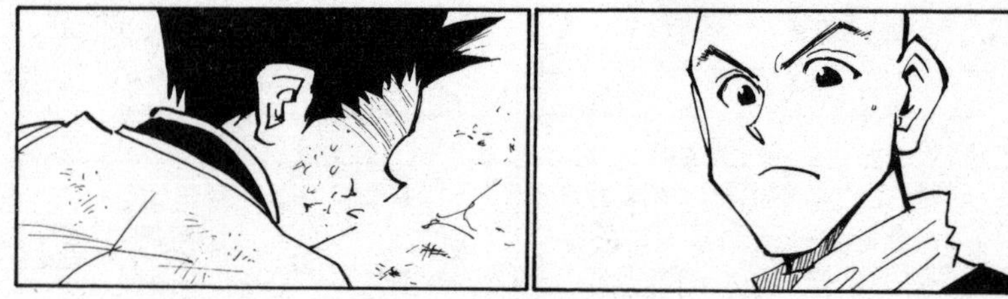

THREE HOURS NOW...
...AND HE'S BEEN BEAT TO A PULP.
GET UP.
UNH...

Y'NEED SOMEBODY T'BEAT ON, SLIMEBALL?!
TRY ME ON FOR SIZE!! C'MON!!

CAN'T TAKE IT? TOO BAD, 'CAUSE...
...IT'S JUST GOING TO GET WORSE.
!
SHUFF

THERE WILL BE NO INTERFERENCE IN A ONE-ON-ONE MATCH.
IF YOU ATTEMPT TO INTERVENE, GON WILL BE DISQUALIFIED.

...!!
IT'S OKAY, LEORIO...
!!
RR RRG
I'M A BIT... BRUISED...
...BUT STILL... GOING STRONG.

WHAM!!

JERK!
!

I'LL BREAK YOUR ARM.

READ
THIS
WAY

I MEAN IT!
GIVE UP, NOW!!
...
NO!!
NO WAY!!
KA-SNAP

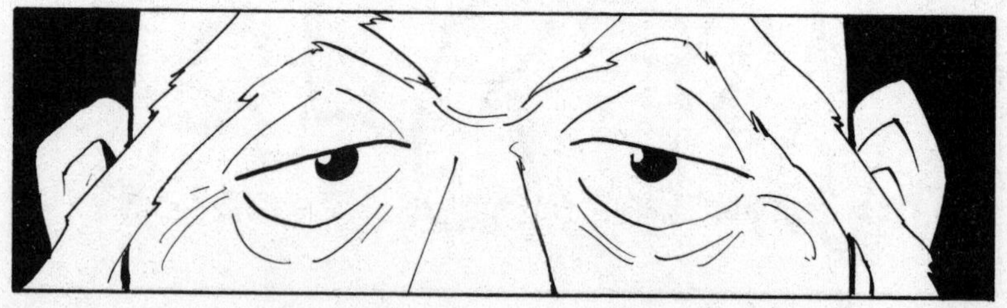

Chapter 34
The First Candidate Accepted?!

...
HE... REALLY *DID IT.*
OKAY...
...THAT'S YOUR *LEFT* ARM OUT OF COMMISSION.

READ THIS WAY
KURAPIKA, I SWEAR ...
...IF THAT CREEP DOES ONE MORE THING, GON FAILS...
...'CAUSE I'M TAKIN' THAT GUY APART!!
YOU?
JUST YOU?
LEORIO...
...GET IN LINE.
YOUR MIND MAY BE BLANK WITH PAIN, BUT HEAR THIS...
...I BELONG TO THE SHINOBI, A CLANDESTINE GROUP.

FROM BIRTH I'VE BEEN SUBJECT TO A STRICT TRAINING PROGRAM, IN ORDER TO MASTER THE SPECIAL SKILLS CALLED NINJUTSU.
I'VE NEVER ONCE, IN THE 18 YEARS SINCE, BROKEN TRAINING.
I'D KILLED BY THE TIME I WAS YOUR AGE.
IT TOOK YOU THAT LONG?
HMPH...
SWIH
THERE IS NO WAY...
SWUH
...YOU CAN TAKE ME IN A FIGHT!
THUM!
TRUST ME, YOUR ONLY OPTION...
...IS TO ADMIT DEFEAT.
GLARE

WHOCK
UFF!
THROB
WOBBLE
THUMP
SPLAT!
THROB
!!
OWWW...!
Y-Y'KNOW... *Y'TALK* TOO DANG MUCH!

AWRIGHT, GON!! PUT ANOTHER ONE IN! MAKE IT HURT!!
MURDER DA BUM !!
YEAH!
SO HE CAN FAIL?
EIGHTEEN? SO YOU'RE ONLY 6 YEARS OLDER THAN ME!
...
ANYWAY, THIS ISN'T ABOUT STRENGTH OR SKILL...
...BUT ABOUT STICKING TO BUSINESS, NO MATTER WHAT!
Heh ...
FWUP
THROB
I LET YOU GET THAT KICK IN...
THROB
THROB
THROB
WHAT?! LIAR!!
YOU DON'T SEEM TO REALIZE I'M..
SNURF
...NOT ADVISING, I'M ORDERING! THERE IS A DIFFERENCE!
BUT MAYBE I'M NOT...
...MAKING THAT CLEAR ENOUGH.

READ THIS WAY

INSTEAD OF A BREAK, I'LL...
...AMPUTATE! LET'S SEE...
ZWIP

...A LEG SHOULD DO IT! IRREPARABLY MAIMED, YOU MAY FINALLY...
...GET MY POINT! SO GIVE UP...
...BEFORE I ACTUALLY MAKE IT!
FWISH
FWISH

THAT'S A PROBLEM!

BWOOONG!!
OF COURSE I DON'T WANT TO LOSE MY LEG!!
BUT I'M AS DETERMINED NOT TO GIVE UP!!

WE GOTTA FIND ANOTHER WAY!
ANOTHER ...?!
YOU'RE IN NO POSITION TO DICTATE TERMS!!

HEH...
HEH HEH
HEH... SORRY.

IT'S A FLAT CHOICE— GIVE UP...
...OR I SLICE OFF YOUR LEG! THAT'S IT!!
I DON'T ACCEPT THAT CHOICE!

AND YOU SHOULDN'T OFFER IT!
EH...?
I BLEED TO DEATH, HE FAILS, RIGHT?
UM...
...YES!

SEE?
THAT'S A PROBLEM...
...FOR BOTH OF US.
...
...

HOW INTERESTING.
GON HAS TAKEN CONTROL.
His will is...
...breath-taking.
HE'S GOT...
... EVERYONE'S ATTENTION.
HANZO'S, TOO...

WHAT IS THIS...?!
WHAT'S CHANGED?! GON'S NOT ANY STRONGER...
...AND HIS ARM HASN'T MAGICALLY HEALED!!
SO HOW IS IT THAT HE'S...
...SUDDENLY IN THE DRIVER'S SEAT?!
GRIT
!!

BWIIING

IT'S JUST NOT SINKING IN, IS IT? IF YOU'RE DEAD...

...YOU'RE DONE... FOR GOOD.
HOWEVER, EVEN IF I KILL YOU...
...I CAN JUST REAPPLY NEXT YEAR!!
THE CHOICE I GIVE YOU REMAINS!!

HE'S RIGHT, GON.
NIMBLE AS YOU ARE MENTALLY...
...YOU LACK THE COMBAT SKILLS.

AND HANZO HAS ALL THAT OVER YOU!!
TUP
IN THE END, IT ALL COMES DOWN TO ABILITY!!

WHY?
WHY STAND NOW?
YOU'D ACE THE EXAM NEXT YEAR!

IS YOUR PRIDE ALL YOU CARE ABOUT?! EVEN MORE THAN YOUR LIFE?!

IS IT SOME KIND OF WEIRD RUSH TO HOLD OUT IN THE FACE OF IMPOSSIBLE ODDS?!

I WANT TO SEE MY DAD.

HE'S A HUNTER...

...ONE OF THE *BEST*, I HEAR.

WE'LL MEET SOMEDAY, I HOPE.

BUT...

VERY WELL, I HEREBY...

VWIT

...GIVE UP THE MATCH.

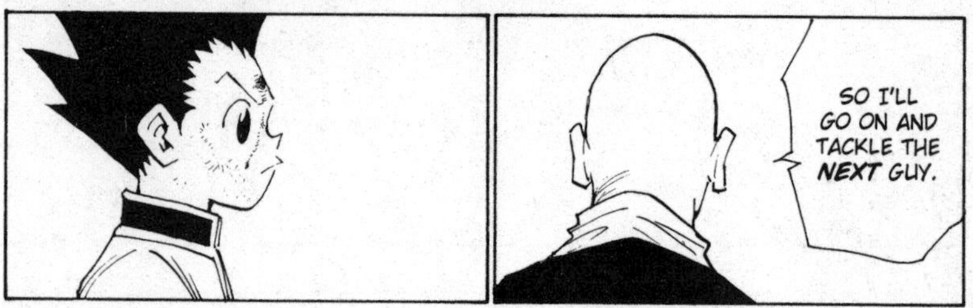

HEY! YOU'RE JUST WALKING AWAY?!

C'MON, WE CAN DO BETTER THAN THAT! WE CAN HAVE A PROPER MATCH!

SNAP

HEH...

WHY AM I NOT SURPRISED?

AND WHY SHOULD I **BOTHER?** YOU **WON'T** GIVE UP! **END OF STORY!**

BUT I **HATE** WINNING LIKE THIS! SO WOULD **YOU!**

WHAT DO YOU **SUGGEST,** THEN?!

YOU AND I CAN FIGURE THAT OUT— **TOGETHER!!**

IN OTHER WORDS...

...EVEN THOUGH **I'M** ALL SET TO SURRENDER, **YOU** WANT US TO FIGURE OUT A WAY TO FIGHT...

...THAT NOT ONLY GIVES YOU A **CHANCE** AGAINST ME, BUT A WAY TO WIN "HONESTLY".

HAVE I GOT THAT RIGHT?!

DREAM ON!!!

READ THIS WAY

OKAY, I'M THE LOSER. ON TO THE NEXT ROUND.
I THINK YOU MAY HAVE A LITTLE PROBLEM ON YOUR HANDS, THOUGH.

THAT'S ONE STUBBORN KID, AND WHEN...
...HE WAKES UP, HE WON'T BE AT ALL HAPPY.
HE MIGHT DELIBERATELY DRAW...
...A DISQUALIFICATION. IF SO, THAT'LL END THE FINALS ON A DECIDEDLY SOUR NOTE.

Haven't we seen this before...?

THROB
THROB
THROB
THROB

Chapter 35

Light and Darkness, part 1

...
OH... HI.
GOOD, YOU'RE AWAKE.

THIS ROOM... WHERE ...?
OOF ...
THE WAITING ROOM NEXT TO THE EXAM HALL.
SCOOOT

OH... RIGHT, I WAS FACING OFF AGAINST HANZO...
YOUR ARM WILL BE *FINE*, BY THE WAY.
THE BREAK WAS CLEAN, AND EASILY SET.
IN FACT, THAT LIMB WILL BE *STURDIER* ONCE IT MENDS.

AND, LEST I FORGET...
SHUP

...*CONGRAT-ULATIONS* ON YOUR WIN.

SATOTZ, I DIDN'T...

DIDN'T WHAT?

IF YOU FEEL IT'S NOT DESERVED, YOU'RE FREE TO THROW AWAY YOUR LICENSE, OR STASH IT SOMEWHERE.
OR EVEN SELL IT, THOUGH IT'S OF NO PRACTICAL USE TO ANYONE ELSE.

THERE ARE ECCENTRICS WHO'D STILL PAY TOP DOLLAR FOR IT.

REALIZE, THOUGH, THAT YOU HAVE NOW PASSED THE EXAM. AND NO ONE WHO PASSES THE EXAM CAN RETAKE IT.

THANKS TO THE ACHIEVEMENTS OF EXISTING HUNTERS, OUR GRADUATES RECEIVE ALL MANNER OF FAVORABLE TREATMENT.
WHICH SPURS NO END OF APPLICANTS SEEKING A LICENSE FOR THE WORST INTENTIONS.

IF IT WEREN'T FOR THEM...
...WE WOULDN'T HAVE TO PUT OUR APPLICANTS THROUGH SUCH A GRINDER.
RUMMAGE
SWUP
FOR A PRO HUNTER, THIS CARD...
...IS THE MOST IMPORTANT THING IN HIS LIFE.
ALL THE SAME, IT'S JUST A SILLY PIECE OF PLASTIC.

HOWEVER YOU BECOME A HUNTER, WHAT MATTERS IS WHAT YOU ACCOMPLISH AS ONE...
...WOULDN'T YOU SAY?

WHAT SORT OF HUNTER ARE YOU?
ME? I RESTORE AND PRESERVE RUINS.

I USED TO FOCUS ON EXCAVATION, FOR THE FAME...
...BUT THE WORK OF A CERTAIN OTHER HUNTER SHOWED ME...

...WHAT WAS REALLY IMPORTANT. HE PAID FOR RESTORATIONS WITH HIS OWN FUNDS, AS WELL AS PUBLIC VIEWING FACILITIES THAT EMPHASIZED PRESERVATION. IT WAS A LOT OF WORK, WITH TREMENDOUS BENEFITS TO THE WORLD. I WAS SHAMED, AND INSPIRED.
THIS HUNTER'S METHODS HAVE NOW BEEN ADOPTED WORLDWIDE AS THE VERITABLE TEXTBOOK ON ARCHEOLOGICAL MANAGEMENT.

THOUGH I'VE NEVER MET HIM, HE'S MY ROLE MODEL.
I WOULD BE HONORED TO MEET HIM ONE DAY, TO THANK HIM.
YOU KNOW THE LURKA RUINS? IF YOU GET THE CHANCE...
...GO SEE THEM. THEY'LL SHOW YOU WHAT I MEAN.
I WILL!

GON...

...THIS IS YOURS. ACCEPT IT. IT REMAINS FOR YOU...
...TO DECIDE WHEN TO USE IT.
THAT'S... FAIR.
I GOT A LOT OF HELP...
...AND OWE A LOT OF FAVORS.

ONCE I'VE RETURNED THEM, I'LL BE READY.

AGAIN, GON...

READ THIS WAY

...AND WHEN HE WAKES UP, HE WON'T BE AT ALL HAPPY.
HUP.
HE MIGHT DELIBERATELY DRAW...
...A DISQUALIFICATION. IF SO, THAT'LL END THE FINALS ON A DECIDEDLY SOUR NOTE.
NOT A PROBLEM.
GON HAS PASSED THE EXAM, AND IS NO LONGER A CONTENDER IN THE FINALS.

READ THIS WAY

WHEN I...
...TORTURE SOMEONE, I KNOW HE'LL DESPISE ME FOR IT.
SO I DON'T SWEAT IT.
?

ANY VICTIM WILL LOOK AT HIS TORMENTOR WITH A VENGEFUL FIRE IN HIS EYES.
EVEN THE MOST DISCIPLINED WARRIOR CAN'T REALLY HIDE HIS HATRED AND RESENTMENT.

BUT THERE, IN GON'S EYES...
...I SAW NONE OF THAT...EVEN AFTER I BROKE HIS ARM.
NONE OF IT REALLY MATTERED TO HIM.

READ THIS WAY

I KINDA *LIKE* THE LITTLE RUNT NOW.

GUESS *THAT'S* WHY I *DECIDED* TO LOSE.

ROUND TWO! KURAPIKA VS. HISOKA!

KILLUA FAILED? WHY?
HE BROKE THE RULES.
THE RULES?
YOU MEAN...?
HE KILLED SOMEONE.

READ THIS WAY

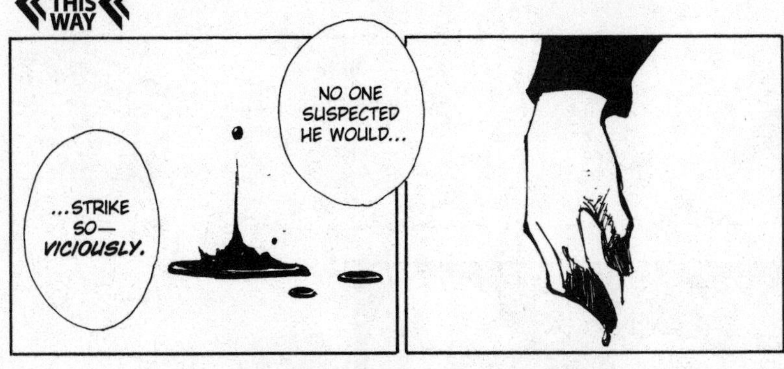
NO ONE SUSPECTED HE WOULD...
...STRIKE SO— *VICIOUSLY.*

IT WAS *QUICK* AND, WE BELIEVE, *INTENTIONAL.*

IT ALL HAPPENED...
...WHILE I WAS *SLEEPING?*
I'LL BREAK IT DOWN FOR YOU.
KURAPIKA WON...
...ROUND TWO.
AFTER A BIT OF TUSSLING...
...HISOKA *WHISPERED* SOMETHING...
...AND THEN *DECLARED DEFEAT.*

READ
THIS
WAY

ROUND THREE WAS HANZO VS. POKKLE.

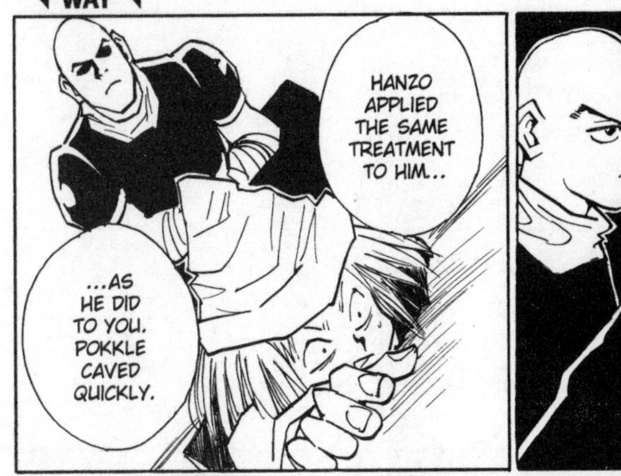
HANZO APPLIED THE SAME TREATMENT TO HIM...
...AS HE DID TO YOU. POKKLE CAVED QUICKLY.

DO YOU WANT WHAT GON GOT? DO YOU? I WON'T HESITATE IN YOUR CASE.
AND THAT WAS THAT.

ROUND FOUR, HISOKA VS. BODORO.

A MOST ONE-SIDED BOUT...
...BUT BODORO WAS STUBBORN.

HISOKA WHISPERED SOMETHING TO HIM...
...AND THIS TIME, EMERGED THE WINNER.

ROUND FIVE, KILLUA VS. POKKLE.
KILLUA **CONCEDED** ON THE SPOT.
SORRY, GOT OTHER FISH TO FRY.
I THINK HE WANTED TO FACE...
...AN OPPONENT UP TO **HIS** STANDARDS.
HOW-EVER ...
ROUND SIX, LEORIO VS. BODORO.
DUE TO BODORO'S INJURIES, LEORIO REQUESTED A POSTPONE-MENT...
...WHICH WAS GRANTED. KILLUA AND GITTARACKUR FOUGHT NEXT.
AND **THIS** WAS WHERE THINGS **DERAILED.**
BEGIN!!

READ THIS WAY

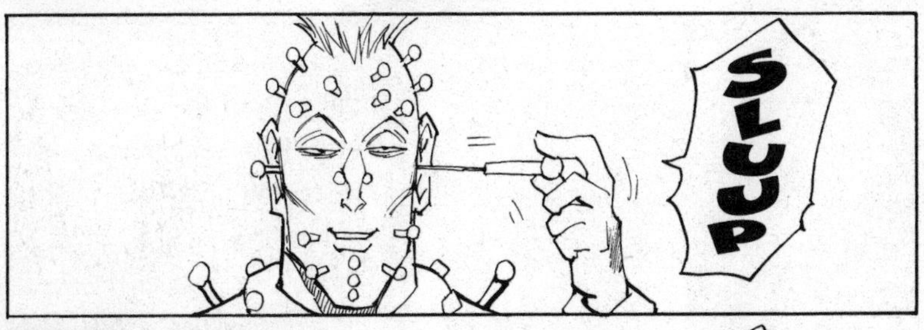

Coming Next Volume...

Killua has given up on being a Hunter, and Gon is sure that family pressure has convinced his friend to give up his dream. Gon is determined to talk some sense into Killua, and drags the rest of the gang along with him. But Killua has retreated behind the impassible gates of his family's stronghold, guarded by a terrible beast that eats all visitors! Can Gon, Kurapika and Leorio make it past the monster, or will their first Hunt be their last?

Available now!

You're Reading in the Wrong Direction!!

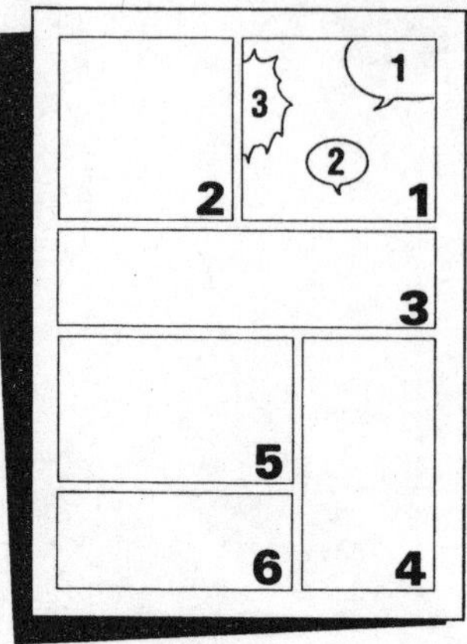

Whoops! Guess what? You're starting at the wrong end of the comic!

...It's true! In keeping with the original Japanese format, **Hunter x Hunter** is meant to be read from right to left, starting in the upper-right corner.

Unlike English, which is read from left to right, Japanese is read from right to left, meaning that action, sound effects and word-balloon order are completely reversed... something which can make readers unfamiliar with Japanese feel pretty backwards themselves. For this reason, manga or Japanese comics published in the U.S. in English have sometimes been published "flopped"–that is, printed in exact reverse order, as though seen from the other side of a mirror.

By flopping pages, U.S. publishers can avoid confusing readers, but the compromise is not without its downside. For one thing, a character in a flopped manga series who once wore in the original Japanese version a T-shirt emblazoned with "M A Y" (as in "the merry month of") now wears one which reads "Y A M"! Additionally, many manga creators in Japan are themselves unhappy with the process, as some feel the mirror-imaging of their art skews their original intentions.

We are proud to bring you Yoshihiro Togashi's **Hunter x Hunter** in the original unflopped format. For now, though, turn to the other side of the book and let the adventure begin...!

–Editor